THE HEARTFULNESS WAY

THE HEARTFULNESS WAY

Heart-Based Meditations for Spiritual Transformation

Daaji

KAMLESH D. PATEL
WITH JOSHUA POLLOCK

juggernaut

JUGGERNAUT BOOKS
C-I-128, First Floor, Sangam Vihar,
Near Holi Chowk, New Delhi 110080, India

First published by Westland in 2018
First published by Juggernaut Books in 2022

10 9 8 7 6 5 4 3 2

P-ISBN: 9789393986245
E-ISBN: 9789393986313

Typeset in Arno Pro by R. Ajith Kumar, Noida

Printed at Thomson Press India Ltd

CONTENTS

Preface

We never know what life has in store for us and what is just around the corner. That is part and parcel of the mystery and beauty of living. I have received many blessings during my six decades on this Earth, and one of those happened while I was a teenager, studying pharmacy in Ahmedabad in India in 1976. Thanks to one of my college pals, I came across Heartfulness meditation, and a few months later was face-to-face with a remarkable man who immediately became my first guru and who guided me in this practice. His name was Ram Chandra, and we called him Babuji.

The effect of the very first Heartfulness meditation on me was so profound that it was clear I had found my direction and anchor in life. But the effect of meeting Babuji was beyond even that—something so precious and subtle in its essence that it defies description. While universes and dimensions have opened in my inner world since that time, it is only one aspect of what has unfolded during these last four decades. What is even more wonderful is the wealth of everyday qualities that have come through Heartfulness practice—qualities such as love, acceptance, humility, service, compassion, empathy, and a higher purpose to existence.

It all starts with the simple act of meditation. Nothing much is required of us as we sit quietly, close our eyes, and focus within on the Source of all existence in our hearts. If we can approach the act of meditation with childlike wonder and innocence, our inner universe unfolds before us naturally. In a heart-based meditation practice, we explore and experience the simplest and purest aspect of our existence: our soul. Everything about it is so natural.

The Heartfulness practices in this book nurture our souls, remove the weeds and mud that keep them hidden, and set free that spark of childlike innocence and wonder that makes life truly meaningful. At the same time, we have to live in the day-to-day world of urban stress, wages and mortgages, careers and relationships. Heartfulness practices help us simplify our responses and navigate our daily lives in an enriching, fulfilling manner.

If you knew there was a practical way to transcend suffering and fly into the sky of hope and contentment, would you be interested? That is exactly what Heartfulness offers—not by removing problems or by shutting them out, but by transforming us from the inside out so that we see the world in a new way, without the filters of our limitations.

In the Heartfulness way, we explore and expand our consciousness, and even go beyond consciousness to uncover true potentiality. I hope you enjoy this book and benefit from what I have learned on this journey of life so far.

Kamlesh D. Patel
January 2018

Introduction

IN AUGUST 2015, as I sat in my home office in Chennai, India, my wife appeared with my phone. 'It's Kamlesh calling from Europe,' she said, laughing. Apparently, our two-year-old daughter had answered the phone and held her own conversation with him for some time before my wife noticed. When I picked up the phone, he said, 'I would like you to write a book about meditation.' I immediately agreed, but I also had a little trepidation. Because Kamlesh has been meditating for over forty years and is a spiritual guide to seekers all over the world, I felt he was far more qualified to write a book on this subject.

When we met weeks later, I said, 'Maybe you should write this book instead.'

He laughed and replied, 'We'll write it together.'

Over the course of two years, we had numerous

wide-ranging discussions in locations throughout India and the US. *The Heartfulness Way* chronicles those conversations.

About twenty years earlier, a fascination with books prompted my interest in meditation. As a teenager, I found myself drawn to the subject of spirituality. I was sure that if I searched long enough through my parents' enormous book collection, I would find some obscure and esoteric text, and from its pages, all the great secrets of the universe would pour out.

First, I encountered the *Tao Te Ching*, penned by the eminent sage Lao Tzu, supposedly at the point of a spear. It mesmerized me with its simplicity and wisdom, and fanned the flames of spiritual craving in my heart. This led me to other books. I poured through the literature of the Buddhists, Taoists, Sufis, Christians, and others. I read Aristotle and Augustine, Emerson and Epicurus. Gradually it dawned on me that through all my reading, I had only learned about the experiences and ideas of others. What about my own? Until this point, all my knowledge was abstract. I had become familiar with so many spiritual ideas, but in a bookish way. I had come across so many terms—*enlightenment, satori, samadhi, illumination*. I needed to find out on my own what these concepts meant, and I knew that this required a practical approach.

I embarked on a mad dash through various practices. I took meditation classes, tried yoga, and studied martial arts. Once, I met a famous Zen master. When he looked at me, I only managed to stammer, 'I've never met a master before.'

'But you will!' he replied.

By then, I was already meditating on a daily basis. However, I did not find meditation to be gratifying. It was a real struggle—a difficult and tedious affair. After a few years of searching, my enthusiasm started to wane. Eventually, I gave up my quest, empty-handed and a little disillusioned.

In August 2002, I met a stranger while standing outside a local shop. In the course of our conversation, I learned that she practised a form of meditation known alternately as *Sahaj Marg* (which means 'natural path' in Hindi) and Heartfulness. She spoke as if the practice of Heartfulness had really changed her life.

Despite my curiosity about this new kind of meditation, I was also a little skeptical. By now, I had become immune to the various claims made about meditation. My own experience of meditation had been different. *Perhaps I just wasn't cut out to meditate,* I thought. Additionally, I suspected that a true path might not be found so easily. I wondered whether finding a capable teacher might involve trekking deep into the Himalayas or travelling to some other remote locale. What are the odds of finding something authentic during a chance encounter on the street? But something else inside me said, 'It's possible …'

Then, one bright September morning, my mother called me. She was in tears. My little sister had just been in a car accident. She was unconscious and on her way to the hospital. Nobody knew if she would live or die, and I was halfway across the country. I could do nothing. Toward midnight, my sister was dead at the age of sixteen.

These are the times when people tend to seek meaning, spirituality, and hope. But I had already done that and come up empty. Nevertheless, I set up a meeting with a Heartfulness trainer named Brian Jones. Brian is a professional artist. We met at his studio, which was filled with paintings in varying stages of completion. Over coffee, I was impressed to learn that all Heartfulness trainers are volunteers, that none of them accept any fee for their service. Brian then invited me into an adjacent room to meditate, or to give me a 'sitting,' as he called it. He motioned me to a chair and took the seat across from me. He explained how to meditate on the heart and said that his role would simply be to meditate along with me and that this would help facilitate my own meditation. He then asked me to close my eyes and said, 'Please start.'

It is difficult to explain what followed. It wasn't until much later that I understood that I had experienced a glimpse of *samadhi*—a state of profound inner equanimity, where you drift beyond yourself, beyond the here and now, beyond everything. When he broke the meditation by saying, 'That's all,' I felt as if I had been yanked out of eternity.

Quietly, we sat in the post-meditative stillness, enjoying its languid beauty. In that moment, I knew that I had experienced something unique—something for which I had been thirsting my whole life. I did not know what that 'something' was, but for the first time in memory, my heart was absolutely joyful and at peace. Later, I would learn that this experience was brought about by something called 'yogic transmission.'

Heartfulness is an integrated approach that consists of three core practices: meditation, cleaning, and prayer. These three practices are supported by yogic transmission, which is the essence of the Heartfulness approach and the key to its transformative potential.

Through meditation, we move from the complexity of mind to the simplicity of heart. Everything starts with the heart. When the heart is at peace, the mind is at rest. When the heart is content, the mind gains insight, clarity, and wisdom. We often think that the heart and mind are two distinct entities that are often in conflict with one another. In Heartfulness meditation, we use the heart to regulate the mind, thus bringing them both into alignment. The two entities unite in meditative togetherness, and we become integrated.

The cleaning method frees us from the various mental and emotional tendencies that often dominate our lives. Through it, we purify our hearts by removing inner heaviness, base qualities, and desires. Gradually, our authentic nature is revealed.

In prayer, we affirm our connection to the spiritual Source within. The act of prayer further evolves into a state of prayerfulness, which beckons us to unite with that Source. It creates an aspiration and a craving that resolves itself in profound meditation.

The Heartfulness practice emerged in India in the early twentieth century. Its progenitor was a yogi named Ram Chandra, whom people called Lalaji. From the very beginning, Lalaji set a tone of inclusiveness, accepting students from any religious and social background, which was rare for his time and place. He himself was steeped in various traditions, which he synthesized and innovated to create a path that could serve an increasingly modernized humanity. Modern seekers have numerous responsibilities and are not equipped to devote themselves exclusively to their spiritual aspirations. Heartfulness proposes a balanced, integrated existence, where life's spiritual and material wings can harmoniously coexist.

Lalaji's spiritual successor was also named Ram Chandra, but was commonly known as Babuji, who perfected the Heartfulness practice, bringing it into its present form and guiding seekers around the world. Babuji's successor was Parthasarathi Rajagopalachari (Chariji), the third guide of the Heartfulness way. When Chariji passed away on 20 December 2014, Kamlesh became the fourth guide in the Heartfulness lineage.

It was my good fortune to have numerous interactions with Chariji when I relocated to India for work in 2008. When I first met him, I immediately remembered what the Zen master had foretold years earlier. However, I would later come to understand that 'meeting the master' is something that happens within, rather than externally.

While living in India, I also met Kamlesh, who was my neighbour and the father of one of my friends. I quickly developed great respect and affection for him. He was one of the most authentic and down-to-earth individuals I had ever known. I remember one instance when his son remarked that one of our apartment complex's security guards always seemed unhappy. 'Maybe he would benefit from meditation,' he said to his father. Kamlesh replied, 'Right now, that man needs bread more than he needs God.'

Kamlesh was born in the northwestern Indian state of Gujarat in 1956. He started Heartfulness practice in 1976, while a student at pharmacy college. After graduating, he moved to the United States and worked as a pharmacist in New York City while continuing his meditation practice. In 2011, Chariji formally nominated him as his spiritual successor, which came to fruition on the sad day of Chariji's passing.

Since then, Kamlesh has completely devoted himself to his spiritual duties, which include guiding the activities of Heartfulness Institute and offering continuous support to seekers from every corner of the world. He eschews all formal titles, but many people refer to him as Daaji, which means 'father's younger brother' in his native Gujarati.

The Heartfulness Way is a series of candid conversations between Daaji and me, in which we explore the practice and principles of Heartfulness. In these conversations, I ask Daaji many questions. Some are questions that I had as a beginner in meditation. Others are questions that I have often been asked in my capacity as a Heartfulness trainer. Still others are questions that sprung naturally to my mind in the course of our discussions.

The Heartfulness Way consists of three parts. Part 1 examines the nature of the spiritual search, and demystifies meditation and yogic transmission.

Part 2 introduces the core practices of Heartfulness: meditation, cleaning, and prayer. It blends foundational knowledge and practical instruction. Each chapter concludes with a step-by-step guide to lead you through these simple practices.

Part 3 is a discussion about the guru's invisible yet vital role in supporting our inner journey.

The Heartfulness Way is an invitation to experience the simple practice that has transformed my life and those of others practising Heartfulness around the world. Of course, no book can ever transform us. A book may give us wisdom, but it cannot make us wise. A book can give us knowledge, but it cannot make us experience the truth of that knowledge. What this book offers is an experiential method that has helped many individuals discover that truth for themselves.

We may seek spirituality in various places, but the spiritual Source can never be found externally. It is a presence that can never be grasped, but only felt. When we do, it is with the heart that we feel it, for the heart is the organ of feeling. To practise Heartfulness is to seek the essence beyond the form. It is to seek the reality behind the ritual. It is to centre oneself in the core of one's heart and find true meaning and contentment there.

Daaji's message to seekers is simple and direct: experience is greater than knowledge. Any good teacher understands this. That is why so many classes have both a lecture and a laboratory module. Daaji often says that in the lecture, you learn the principles, but in the lab you experiment and gain practical experience. I invite you to make your own heart your lab and the practice of Heartfulness your experiment.

In any experiment, there is an experimenter, there is a subject to be experimented upon, and there is a result. In the spiritual experiment, all three roles belong to you. You are the experimenter, you are the subject of the experiment, and you are its result. With such an experiment, there is never any finality, but only an ongoing process of discovery. That is the joy and wonder of Heartfulness.

Joshua Pollock
January 2018

Part One

Why Heartfulness

1

The Seeker's Journey

ENTERING DAAJI'S APARTMENT in Chennai, India, I found him relaxing on an indoor swing. As I walked toward him, a warm smile appeared on his face.

'What's up, brother?' he said, extending his hand to shake mine. I sat across from him. A relative appeared from the next room and offered me tea. Daaji intervened.

'Give him coffee,' he said. 'He'll enjoy it more.' It was the truth.

The first thing people often notice about Daaji is his poise. It is a rare quality, which seems to touch anyone in his presence. His words are well placed and deliberate. Generally, he says only what is necessary to convey the bare essence. It then becomes incumbent upon the listener to further explore and expand the idea. Periods of silence often punctuate his speech. In such moments, a person can understand many things—things that are even more important than his teachings. In this situation, a questioner tends to become inwardly content and forget all their questions. As Daaji's interviewer, this was now my fear! However, I instead found a new dynamic emerging between us. Our conversation flowed unabated, and he answered every question enthusiastically and in great depth.

'So, you're here with questions,' said Daaji.

'Yes, but I'll start with just one,' I said. 'Why meditate?'

'Why not?' he replied with a chuckle. 'Well, each person's reason will be different. In life, our goals tend to correspond to our personal needs and tastes. For instance, one person joins a gym in order to lose weight. Another person wants six-pack abs. Yet both visit the same gym. I have observed a pattern in my interactions with meditators around the globe. Initially, people tend to approach meditative practice with a wide spectrum of aims. For example, many people suffer from a stressful lifestyle. They want to find a way to relax. Someone else wants to reduce blood pressure. Another person seeks mental clarity. Others want emotional balance. But when they start meditation, they soon begin to harvest benefits that far exceed these aims. Often, people are surprised to report a profound sense of spiritual well-being—a state reflected by the presence of inner joy and even bliss. It is as if a hungry person asks for a small scrap of food, but then, someone surprises them with a banquet!

'What's more, these results are palpable and immediate. We can experience them after a single meditation. In that case, what would happen if you meditated a second and a third time? Imagine the cumulative effect of numerous meditations!'

'But does meditation also address our original aims?' I asked.

'It addresses them without specifically targeting them,' he said. 'Meditation simply normalizes your inner state, whatever it may be. A stressed person may meditate and say, "Meditation relaxes you." A person with disturbed emotions may meditate and say, "Meditation calms your emotions." An angry and bitter person may meditate and say, "Meditation opens your heart. It makes you loving."

'Hearing these varied responses can confuse

us! *What does meditation actually do?* we think to ourselves.'

'So what *does* it do?' I asked.

'It creates naturalness,' said Daaji. 'As you proceed toward naturalness, that which is unnatural in you starts to disappear. There may be a thousand varieties of unnaturalness, but there is only one naturalness. Attaining that, we resolve a thousand complaints.

'Why meditate? The answer is complex because our goals change as we progress. Today's reason is different from tomorrow's. And that is as it should be! As we meditate, wisdom grows. We better understand what we are and what we should be. And meditation is the vehicle that takes us on this infinite journey.'

'If the journey is infinite, can we ever arrive?' I asked.

'Where?' he said with a laugh. 'The moment you think, *Yes, I have made it,* you stop growing. You stop moving. Evolution can never stop. We must always be willing to change. We must be ready to go to the next step, whatever it may be. Then, having reached that step, we must be prepared and flexible enough to go even further.'

'But spiritual literature is replete with examples

of figures who were supposedly perfect beings,' I said.

'Do you think they would describe themselves in such a way?' he asked. 'In mathematics, there is something called an *asymptote*. It's a line that is approached by a curve, which intersects the line at infinity. That curve moves infinitely closer to the line, but the two never meet. They only get closer and closer. A highly advanced aspirant is like that curve. She forever approaches the destination without ever arriving. At any given moment, she is both infinitely close and infinitely far from the goal. Yet, she keeps moving. As long as the aspirant exists, the journey will be infinite.'

'What are we moving toward?' I asked.

'From selfishness toward selflessness,' he said. 'From the reactive mind to the responsive heart; from imprisonment in the folds of ego to freedom from ego; from the here and now to eternal, timeless existence; from worshipping forms to formlessness; from contraction to expansion; from restlessness to peacefulness; from the superficial to the authentic; from insistence to acceptance; from imbalance to balance; from darkness to light; from heaviness to lightness; from grossness to subtlety; from the periphery to the core of the Being, the Source, the Higher Self.

'You see, the purpose of meditation is to transform us. Transformation is the purpose of religion, too. It is also the purpose of self-help and psychiatry. Yet, whenever we try to change ourselves in any way, we tend to encounter tremendous forces of inertia that prevent us from achieving our goals.

'Of course, there is a lot of help available. There is no lack of great teachings—especially in this modern age! At the click of a mouse, we can access the wealth of nearly any tradition. We can view the latest scientific research on so many subjects. It's the age of information. Yet, information can only do so much to help us.'

Daaji laughed and said, 'I am reminded of an old couplet: "Worms ate up thousands of books but did not receive a certificate of erudition."

'That's what a bookworm is. No matter how much knowledge they gain, it doesn't make them any wiser! Knowledge cannot change us, you see. For example, we all know that patience is a virtue, but is knowledge enough to make us patient? Similarly, we all know the value of love. The great teachers of the world have all spoken of it. However, to know about love and to feel and express it are entirely different matters!

'What do we learn from this? If teachings alone were sufficient, we would all be transformed by now. After all, many great personalities have come before us and left great teachings behind. Yet, the world remains as it is. Great teachings are not enough. Knowledge is not enough.

'You may believe in the omnipresence of God, for instance, but do you *feel* that constant presence in your life? If not, how does this belief help you? It may give you comfort, but being comforted by a belief is no substitute for experiencing the reality behind it.'

Just then, someone entered the room and called us for lunch.

'Come,' said Daaji. 'Let's eat.'

We sat at the table, but found that the food wasn't ready. Apparently, there had been some miscommunication. Daaji laughed and said, 'See, this is what I'm talking about. You can't satisfy a person's hunger with the promise of food. Neither can mere belief satiate a craving heart.'

Lunch arrived after a while, and we ate in silence. Then, Daaji spoke.

'Through meditation, we go within and connect with something higher. Therefore, we can find it wherever we are. We need not make pilgrimages.

We need not change our dress, our habits, or our names. We need not do anything except close our eyes and sit quietly in meditation. That is how we gain practical spiritual experience.

'Experience is what differentiates spirituality from religion. Belief without experience is hollow. It's too abstract. In worldly life, most people understand this. For instance, science classes have both a lecture and a lab component. In the lecture, you understand the principles, but it is in the lab that you see them in action. You become practically familiar with them. Your secondhand knowledge gains the backing of firsthand experience.

'In spiritual matters, however, people tend to be more conservative. They are uncomfortable with firsthand knowledge and rely on the teachings of others. However, a time comes when the heart demands personal experience. Knowledge cannot satisfy that demand. Belief cannot satisfy it. So, they embark upon a spiritual search. Please don't mistake this as a criticism of religious belief. Religion is a foundation, but what is a foundation, anyway? We must build upon it. A religious teaching may be true, but it matters little unless you have realized that truth for yourself. You see, it is not enough for a teaching to be true. It must be true *for you*.

'Truth must be realized practically, and meditation is the means. When we lack practical experience, the various religions often appear to speak different languages. Then, we see only Christians, Buddhists, Hindus, Muslims, and so many others. In an effort to bridge the gaps, we may strive to learn about each religion. Yet, that knowledge can make them seem even more different from one another! We observe how Christians seek the kingdom of heaven, Buddhists strive for *nirvana,* Hindus pursue liberation and the state of *Aham Brahmasmi* (I am Brahman), and Sufis strive for *fana-e-fana* (death of death) and *baqua-e-baqua* (life of life).

'*Surely they can't all speak of the same truth,* we think. *If one is right, the rest must be wrong.*

'Now we argue. We fight about which God is the true God. We fight over which philosophy is the true philosophy. We debate the legitimacy of the founders. Some people get fed up and become atheists. They think that all the religions must be wrong!

'However, when you meditate and actually experience some of these states, you realize that *they are all the same.* You can no longer be exclusive. You can no longer claim that only your tradition is correct. Instead, you become inclusive and accepting of all perspectives. What is there to fight about?

'Therefore, I always suggest that whatever your tradition may be, please stay with it—*but meditate also*. Meditation will help you go deeper and discover its essence. Then you find that all religions have the same essence. It's like that famous line from the Rigveda: 'The Reality is one; the learned speak of this in many ways.'

Then Daaji made one of his characteristic U-turns.

'Yet, as compelling as our meditative experiences are, they don't always succeed in transforming us,' he said. 'Our experiences may be profound. They may be highly enjoyable. Yet, personal experience rarely translates into personal change. Does a state of rapture automatically make us kind? Does ecstasy make us loving?' He shook his head.

'Then what is the point of experience?' I asked.

'Well, when you want a donkey to move, you have to show it some green grass,' he said, smiling.

'So it's just a matter of incentive,' I said.

'If we didn't have phenomenal experiences in meditation, I don't think anybody would meditate,' he said. 'Meditation transforms us, but we have to have a reason to keep meditating.'

'But I think our experiences do more than encourage us to keep going,' I said. 'They also teach us something.'

'Yes, but that doesn't mean that we learn from them!' Daaji retorted. 'But through meditation, we do change. You see, meditative practice works at deeper levels of our being. Knowledge and experience only work at the conscious level. That is not enough. Our thoughts, attitudes, emotions, and habits have roots in the infinite vastness of the subconscious. What's more, our subliminal thoughts are more powerful than the thoughts we consciously entertain. This is one of the reasons that we fail when restricting our efforts at change to the conscious level. We can change deliberate actions, but how to change subconscious action? When we are barely even aware of something, can we change it? This is our biggest hurdle when trying to affect meaningful change in our lives. A true change agent cannot work at the superficial level alone, but must be effective at all levels of our being. It must be holistic.

'A sound meditative practice fills that gap in our efforts. It works at the deepest levels, activating the dormant evolutionary forces within and propelling us on an evolutionary path. Then, change happens on its own.

'Often, it happens in spite of us! We do not know why we feel so happy. We don't know why we feel so light. Our family, friends, and colleagues take notice. In fact, we now become a transformational presence in their lives as well. We breathe love. We walk love. We talk and live love.

'You see, we're talking about how knowledge and experience both fail us. However, with the added practical element of meditation, they both become extremely useful.'

'Because the knowledge we gain through meditation comes firsthand?' I asked.

'Of course,' said Daaji. 'But meditation also converts secondhand knowledge into something useful. When reading spiritual literature, for instance, we now find that it resonates with our own experience. It also clarifies our experience. Then, it can pull us up to a higher level of understanding.

'With practice, we also start to learn from our experiences. Previously, we unconsciously resisted change, and our experiences went to waste. But over time, meditative practice wipes that inner resistance away. Like a horse that runs at the shadow of a whip, all we need now is the mere hint of an experience. That's enough to trigger an inner change. We become like an object in outer space, where you only need to give it a tap, and it keeps going and going. There's no resistance, you see. Our experiences now have the same effect. They only need to tap you, and you become ennobled.'

'What are our experiences really trying to tell us?' I asked.

'Experiences reflect our inner nature,' said Daaji. 'For instance, when I'm angry, I have a negative experience. That anger prevents me from having the kind of experiences that I would prefer to have. When I'm jealous, there is another negative experience. But when I'm loving and generous, it's a beautiful experience. And the intensity of that beauty depends upon the extent of my love and generosity.'

'So they show you which direction to move in?' I asked.

'Yes,' said Daaji. 'They are indicators. When I am like *this*, my experience will be like *that*. When I am like *that*, my experience will be like *this*. And due to certain meditative practices, I am able to change as a result of this understanding.'

'So really, the role of experience hasn't changed much from what it was before we meditated,' I said. 'It is still like the green grass one shows to the donkey because its role is to encourage us in a certain direction.'

'Yes,' said Daaji. 'But now, experience becomes effective because you've removed the donkey's stubbornness!'

'Our inner resistance,' I said.

'Yes,' said Daaji. 'And a time comes when there is no more donkey, either. You see, I eventually realize that there is one single factor that affects all my experiences: the way I handle my ego. The higher my egotism, the worse my experience is. The more humble and insignificant I am, the better my experience is. It's a simple formula! Then, one day, a light bulb goes on in my head: How would it be if I were to become a total zero—if I were to become *nothing*?'

'And meditation facilitates this, too,' I said.

'Yes,' said Daaji. 'Now, the only kind of change that I find in myself pertains to whether there is more of me or less of me. Conversely, we can ask the question of whether there is more of God or less of God. You see, the more *I* am there, the less He is there, and the less of *me* there is, the more His presence manifests. It now becomes a question of being and non-being.'

'Ah, that's what you meant about the donkey disappearing!' I said.

Daaji nodded.

'When I am dissolved in the Ultimate Source, it is absolute bliss,' he continued. 'Rather, I become bliss. And when I become bliss, how can I experience it? It's like a raindrop that falls into the ocean. There is no more drop. It has become the ocean, you see.

'That's why mystical traditions fall silent in the end. They cannot express the final state, which is so sublime and perfect and balanced.

'And could a person who has attained this state ever be selfish? Could they be violent? The world faces many challenges. Some are political, others are social. Some are economic, others are environmental. In all cases, humanity suffers. But the world's problems are very simple. They are the lack of love between human beings, the lack of compassion, of tolerance, of humility, and of acceptance. They are the arrogance, hatred, and violence that have polluted human hearts. They are prejudice and intolerance. If a person has no peace in their heart, there can be no peace around them. Such a person will always find reasons to argue and fight. Only when a person's own heart is peaceful can their interactions be peaceful.

'How to solve the problem of hatred? Is there

any political solution? Can love and acceptance be legislated and enforced? Can any law change the human heart? The heart only changes when it decides to change. And that is a personal choice that every person must make for themselves. We cannot enforce it upon them. We can only inspire them and offer them the tools.

'Therefore, rather than trying to transform others, let us devote ourselves to our own transformation. As for others, let us be non-demanding of them. Let us be content to love them as they are, to accept them as they are, and to be ever ready to serve them as we would the members of our own family. This is the humanity that the world sorely needs.

'Only love can make it possible to accept another person's flaws. Have you ever seen a mother give up on her children? Even if her child constantly misbehaves, gets thrown out of school or worse, the mother remains by their side, even after everyone else is fed up. This is due to the mother's love. Where there is love, there is acceptance. Where there is love, there is forgiveness. Where there is love, there is compassion. Love is the root of every noble quality. Therefore, when there is love, do you need any other quality? When love is present, acceptance, forgiveness, and compassion all become redundant. Love alone is sufficient. No other quality is required. We all know this. The great teachers of the past and present have all said so. But if teachings were enough, wouldn't we be transformed by now?'

2

Demystifying Meditation

THE PRACTICE OF meditation forms an integral part of many contemplative traditions. It is said to be the most effective way to approach Divinity, transcending both ritual and belief. Rituals, the actions we undertake at the physical level of existence, remain at the physical level. Belief remains at the mental level. To transcend both and arrive at a spiritual state of being, we must take the help of something that belongs to the higher, spiritual level of existence. This is the approach we take in Heartfulness meditation. To better understand it, I decided to start at the beginning.

'What is meditation?' I asked Daaji.

He took out his pen and drew a diagram.

'The vertical axis represents a spectrum between

the focused mind and the unfocused mind,' he said. 'A focused mind settles on one thought and remains there. It is single-pointed. Conversely, the unfocused mind wanders from topic to topic. It thinks many thoughts, and its attention jumps here and there. Between these two extremes, there is a middle ground. Most of the mind's activity occurs there, in that middle ground.

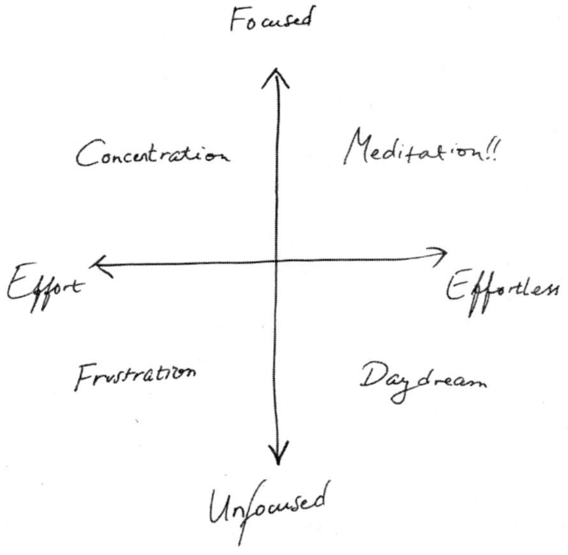

'Here is another polarity: effort and effortlessness. That's the horizontal axis. The effortless mind is relaxed and at ease. On the other side is the effortful mind, which cannot be at ease. It struggles to think, to comprehend, and to concentrate.

'Different combinations of these two spectrums result in certain states of mind. Here, we have daydreaming, frustration, concentration, and meditation. Let's understand the meditative mind. As you can see, it is a mixture of focus and effortlessness. It is to be immersed in one thought, but *effortlessly* so.'

'Can it be any thought?' I asked.

'Yes,' said Daaji.

'But in that case, everybody already meditates!' I said.

'That's what I'm saying,' said Daaji, with a chuckle. 'There is no question of having to learn a new skill. We all know how to meditate. We do it every day.

'For example, a businessman meditates upon a business venture. As he drives his car, he meditates upon that. As he goes to sleep at night, he meditates upon it. Perhaps someone is in love with him. As she goes through her routine, she meditates upon him. As she brushes her teeth, she meditates upon him. She goes to the grocery store, but she meditates upon him the whole time. Meanwhile, she passes a musician in the store. His mind is busy thinking of music. He also meditates. There is even a term called premeditated murder, where the perpetrator meditates on how to perfectly execute his dark plans!'

'If everybody already meditates, then what's so profound about meditation?' I asked.

'What makes it profound is the idea that we explore through meditation,' said Daaji. 'That idea is our object of meditation.

'Our object of meditation makes all the difference. A profound object gives us a profound consciousness. A mundane object gives us a mundane consciousness. A temporary object makes our meditative state of mind temporary. A profound, changeless object makes our meditation permanent. Different objects create different effects, you see.'

'How can we achieve a meditative state that is both permanent and profound?' I asked.

'Effortless focus upon a profound object,' said Daaji. 'For that, we must practice. Without a mother, there can be no baby, and without the practice of meditation, there is no meditative state.'

'I have found that new aspirants are often nervous about trying meditation,' I said. 'They think they will have trouble handling their thoughts.'

'Many say that the mind's nature is to be restless,' said Daaji. 'They say that its natural state is one of disturbance. I disagree. In fact, I would like to dispel that notion.'

'Why is the idea of difficulty so entrenched?' I asked him.

'Many established teachers have espoused this view,' said Daaji. 'In my opinion, they perform a disservice to the cause. If you believe the mind to be inherently unstable, it becomes your enemy. And what do you do with enemies?'

'You fight them,' I answered.

'And so meditation becomes a battle,' he said. 'It becomes an exercise in suppressing the mind. But have your thoughts and emotions ever prevented you from enjoying a good film?'

'No,' I said.

'Have they ever stopped you from enjoying a delicious meal?'

'No again,' I said.

'And why not?' he pressed.

'A film draws your attention,' I said. 'A good meal draws your attention. Then, you don't notice such things.'

'Exactly,' said Daaji. 'When something draws your attention and holds it there, you become unmindful of unwanted thoughts. You only need to give your mind something to sink its teeth into—something really absorbing. Then you will observe just how naturally it stabilizes, how effortlessly it focuses.

'However, we do not seem to have much control over this. Some objects attract the mind, and some simply do not! For example, if your child has been deeply absorbed in his studies all day, you might feel happy. He is engaged in a positive activity. But if you realize that he has been playing video games for nine hours straight, you might start to worry. In both cases, your child exhibits an enormous capacity to focus. But your concern is the *object* upon which he is focused. You are concerned about where his interests lie.

'You see, we do not suffer from an inability to focus. We focus effortlessly upon our interests. But can we choose our interests? It seems that certain objects simply appeal to us more than others. The reason is the impressions that we carry in our consciousness—but we will explore that topic another time. Anyway, when something appeals to you, you become almost enraptured. You are totally focused. It is only when an object does not interest you that you must make efforts to concentrate.

'For instance, what happens when you read a book on a subject that does not speak to your heart? Your mind wanders every second sentence, right? Eventually, you realize that you have no idea what you have just read. You scan back in the text until things start to look familiar. To finish the book, you really have to concentrate!'

'Interest succeeds where force does not,' I said.

'Right,' said Daaji. 'If you have keen interest in a project, you will certainly succeed. If you are not interested, you struggle. Without interest, any activity becomes a drag. Unless the mind finds an idea attractive, it is averse to stay on that topic. It would rather focus on something else.'

'Concentration and focus are not the same thing, are they?' I remarked.

'True focus is effortless,' he replied. 'It happens naturally. It is only when it doesn't happen on its own that we have to make efforts. That is what concentration is—the attempt to focus.

'We define meditation as thinking about one thing continuously. Therefore, many people mistake it for concentration. But meditation is not concentration. Concentration is forceful, while meditation is effortless, involving no force at all.

'In concentration, you have to marshal your mind. You focus on a single idea to the exclusion of all the other ideas that you would prefer to be thinking about! The more deeply you concentrate, the more exclusive your awareness becomes. At its highest pitch, your entire awareness focuses on a single point, excluding all else.

'This requires effort! It is not easy to arrest the flow of thoughts. The mind has a natural momentum. It wants to go in a certain direction, but you are forcing it to go elsewhere. It is like trying to divert a rushing river. Even if you do manage to wrestle your mind into submission, you then have to hold it there! The moment you relax your efforts, it bounces back, like a tightly coiled spring. How long can you maintain such intensity of effort?'

'Even though some people equate meditation with concentration, they also say that meditation should be relaxing,' I said. 'They say that it should give us peace.'

'Can meditation be relaxing or peaceful when we are applying so much effort to concentrate?' asked Daaji. 'So let us forget about concentration. For worldly matters, it may be necessary, but it fails entirely in the spiritual realm.'

'But we define meditation as a state of focus,' I reminded him.

'*Effortless* focus,' Daaji corrected. 'In such a state, your mind naturally settles on one thought. This happens by itself, when an object is able to attract and hold your attention. When your attention is thus harnessed, you are in a state known as *absorption*. That is another word for the meditative state of mind.

'However, "attraction" is double-edged! It is another word for desire, you see.'

'What is desire, really?' I asked.

'Desire is the soul's misdirected urge for completion,' said Daaji. 'The soul craves union with its original Source. That is the real desire—the big desire! Until we know where to look, we tend to seek fulfillment externally instead.

'I'll tell you a story. One day, an ant was crawling along a leaf, when a sparrow landed next to her. "What amazing sights you must see when you fly so high in the sky," sighed the ant. "I only ever see twigs and leaves and pebbles. Please tell me what you see from up there."

"Well," said the sparrow, "I can see the whole forest in a single glance, and in the distance, I can even see the ocean."

"What is the ocean?" asked the ant.

"In the ocean, there is so much water that it has no end," said the sparrow.

"The ant had only ever seen raindrops and droplets of dew.

"*I would like to see this ocean!* thought the ant. "Which direction is the ocean?" she asked the sparrow.

"Oh, it is that way," said the sparrow, pointing his wing.

"Thank you," said the ant, and she set off. She walked for hours and hours. Finally, she encountered a mud puddle. The ant looked to see if she could see the other side, but as far as she could see, there was only water.

"At last, I have reached the ocean!" said the ant.

'That is the situation in which we find ourselves,' laughed Daaji. 'We mistake the ephemeral for the eternal, the finite for the infinite, the mud puddle for the infinite ocean. We seek fulfillment in various objects. However, the satisfaction we derive is limited and temporary. Really, it makes us feel even emptier inside. This is because we lack contact with our inner Source of contentment. Without such contact, we have little choice but to try to fulfill that deeper need in other ways.

'For instance, suppose that your daughter is crying on a long car trip. Then you pass by an ice cream parlor and think, *This will stop her from crying.* You stop and get her ice cream, and she is happy. She is totally and effortlessly absorbed in the ice cream cone. Her mind settles. Really, she is in a state of meditation. The ice cream solves the problem of her dissatisfaction, but it is only a fleeting solution, you see. Afterward, you will have to find a new way to keep her mind occupied. Furthermore, you have conditioned her mind. You have offered ice cream as a solution for its restlessness. Now, she will be more likely to ask for ice cream the next time she feels unsettled. She will certainly request it on your next drive, even if it is a very short one.'

'So, no more ice cream, I guess,' I said.

'No, no, she will never forgive me!' said Daaji.

But I was referring to myself.

'With a limited object of meditation, your meditation provides only limited fulfillment,' he continued. 'With a temporary object of meditation, your fulfillment is temporary. Afterward, you become restless all over again. If you really enjoy your state of absorption, you also seek its repetition.

'In so doing, you create a cycle of fulfillment and lack. If you like ice cream, your mind gravitates toward it. If you prefer whiskey, your mind goes that way instead. Your mind pursues whatever attracts it. Then, we become caught in a cycle of desire and fulfillment. Until we fulfill that desire, we are unstable and restless. After fulfilling it, we again become unstable and restless. We become like pendulums, swinging between lack and fleeting happiness. The more desires we have, the more difficult they are to fulfill. Even when we feel fulfilled in one area, we remain unsatisfied in other ways.

'Furthermore, whenever we don't get what we have become conditioned to require, we become even more unhappy and unfulfilled than we were before. Our mental stability now depends upon the fulfillment of these desires, so we become insistent. "I *must* have this new car!" you say, and it's true. For the sake of your mental stability, you must have it. You have trained yourself to be restless without it, to be unhappy without it. That is the first problem. The second problem is that by repeatedly fulfilling a particular desire, you develop tolerance to that fulfillment.

'One day, I discovered that one of the

pharmacists I employed was addicted to a certain drug. He took doses that would make a normal man collapse, but he was still on his feet, working. He had developed a tolerance to the effects of the drug. With repeated fulfillment of a desire, our dependence increases, but so does our tolerance. We depend more and more upon its fulfillment while deriving less and less satisfaction from it. As a result, we become even more unsettled and dissatisfied.

'What the mind truly craves is permanence. It is not happy with limitation. It is not content with temporary states of happiness. It seeks *infinity*, a fulfillment to end all fulfillments. It seeks to fulfill that desire which, when fulfilled, marks the end of all desire. In short, the mind seeks not merely meditation, but endlessness in meditation. That is true meditation, profound meditation.

'So there is nothing wrong with desire,' Daaji continued, 'but fulfill your real desire. Fulfill the big one. Just as a big fish swallows up the smaller fish, the biggest desire subsumes the smaller ones. In that perfect fulfillment, we attain perfect peace.'

'You're talking about desire and attraction,' I said. 'However, many of the thoughts and emotions to which our minds seem to gravitate are not pleasant.'

'That's true,' said Daaji. 'Attraction does not mean that we like something. Not at all. Rather, it means that the mind gravitates toward it—whether we want it to or not. You see, the other side of desire is fear—aversion, revulsion. For instance, we want to live, and we fear death. They are two sides of the same coin. And as much as we tend to focus on what we want, we also brood over what we do not want. At times, the mind meditates on the positive, and at other times, it gets absorbed in the negative.

'On the negative side, the mind may gravitate toward a discomforting thought, a painful memory, or a difficult emotion. It can even be physical pain. These mental objects are like whirlpools, sucking our attention toward them.

'In fact, all the objects that draw our attention are like whirlpools. It doesn't matter if we feel positive or negative about them. We may try to swim away from them, but we swim against heavy currents. When we are so focused on the thing we want to escape from, its attraction actually becomes stronger. The power of a thought grows to the extent that we give it our attention, you see.

'For instance, a boy sees a girl and goes crazy over her. His mind zeroes in on her. He can't stop thinking about her, and he is also happy to think about her. But what if he is already a married man?'

'Then he's in trouble,' I said.

'The thought of that girl is like a whirlpool. He is inexorably drawn in her direction. Yet, he knows that he cannot allow himself such an indulgence. So, with great effort, he battles the current of his attraction. His mind wants to settle on the thought of her. It is trying to settle, but it is settling on the wrong thing.

'We often become trapped in loops of thought that are not useful to our lives or the lives of others. In fact, these loops of thought can become destructive forces in our lives. Therefore, we have to regulate the mind. We achieve this by practising meditation. And we must practise in such a way that our minds are naturally attracted toward a useful object—a transformational object. That is the benefit that a sound method can confer. The way meditation regulates the mind is by orienting it toward the ultimate Source of contentment.'

'So the object of meditation is extremely important,' I commented.

'Yes, the object determines the effect that our meditation will have upon us,' he said. 'Whether you drink water or whiskey, the act of drinking is the same. The effect is only different because the object is different. Similarly, no matter which object you meditate upon, the act of meditation is the same. It's just that different objects lead to different outcomes. A limited object produces a limited effect. What sort of effect would an unlimited object produce? The idea baffles the mind, but it does not baffle the heart. The heart is intuitive. It does not share the mind's many limitations.'

'What is the unlimited object?' I asked.

'The Source,' said Daaji. 'It is Divinity itself—the original wellspring. To seek Divinity with the mind is to seek it externally. Then, it becomes too cerebral, too abstract. If we try to concentrate, we find nothing upon which to concentrate. If we try to grasp it, it eludes us. It is something that must be found within. When its refreshing breeze first reaches us, it comes through feeling.

'Thinking is narrow, but feeling is broad. It is holistic. It encompasses thinking, but it is beyond thinking. It encompasses all our faculties, but it is beyond them, too. Through feeling, deeper truths are revealed. Divinity cannot be known, you see, but its presence can be felt.

'And can you feel that presence with your

liver or in your heels? Can you feel it with your shoulders or your elbows? The heart is the organ of feeling, and so it is with the heart that we feel it. Therefore, the heart is where we must seek it, and this is why we meditate upon the heart. Here ends our journey in the realm of knowledge, concepts, and forms.'

'How does meditation help us realize this inner presence?' I asked. 'How does it help us unite with it?'

'This is explained well in Patanjali's *Yoga Sutras*,' said Daaji.

The *Yoga Sutras*, often attributed to the sage Patanjali, are an ancient teaching that elucidate certain foundational principles of yoga. Although many people associate the term 'yoga' with a set of physical exercises, that is only one branch of yoga. Yoga is also a meditative approach, the purpose of which is to unite the individual with the universal Source. This aspect of yoga is the subject of the *Yoga Sutras*, in which Patanjali presents a path consisting of eight parts, or steps, known collectively as *ashtanga yoga*. The eight steps are:

1. Yama
2. Niyama
3. Asana
4. Pranayama
5. Pratyahara
6. Dharana
7. Dhyana
8. Samadhi

'All eight steps of the *Yoga Sutras* are important,' said Daaji, 'and we'll discuss each of them in due course. For now, though, I would like to focus on the last four steps: pratyahara, dharana, dhyana, and samadhi. These four steps describe the process by which we enter into the depths of meditation. The steps are distinct from one another, but they are not separate. Rather, they flow into one another. They are four aspects of a single movement—a journey into the depths of our being.

'Let's start with the fifth step, which is pratyahara. Pratyahara means "self-withdrawal". It is to turn inward, to withdraw ourselves from the many distractions that surround us and centre ourselves within. Most of the time, our focus is external. Our awareness is generally limited to whatever we can perceive through the five senses.

We hear, we see, we touch, we smell, we taste, and that's about it. There is nothing wrong with this external orientation. It is vital to our survival. Our senses are a navigation system, you see. They help us secure life's basic necessities: food, shelter, clothing, et cetera.

'However, we tend to go overboard with this material aspect of life. We may achieve material abundance. We may receive the love and admiration of others. But such things cannot fulfill us at the deepest levels. They cannot truly satisfy the heart. No matter how much we achieve or acquire, we still find that we lack something essential. Eventually, we realize that fulfilling our material desires does not make us fulfilled. The heart pines for something else entirely—something far deeper.'

'You spoke about this already,' I said. 'You mentioned the soul's urge for completion, the urge to unite with its Source.'

'Yes,' said Daaji. 'But that concept is too intellectual. It's too abstract to resonate with our hearts. That fundamental urge for union is something that we must discover in ourselves. Until we do, it generally gets misdirected, and we continue to hunt inner fulfillment on the material plane. Our search remains external, and we remain preoccupied with acquiring and consuming things.

'We easily become addicted to constant intake, to constant stimulus. For example, you see so many people checking their smartphones every few seconds! In meditation, we temporarily withdraw ourselves from such things. We take a break from the constant movement of life. We turn away from its enticements, its anxieties, and its stresses. In other words, we stop searching outside ourselves. That is pratyahara. In pratyahara, we go within. The Bhagavad Gita provides us with an instructive image: "When the yogi withdraws his senses from their objects, just like the turtle withdrawing its limbs from all directions, his consciousness is well established." We become centered within, you see.

'If you want to understand pratyahara even further, examine its Sanskrit etymology. We form the word "pratyahara" from two Sanskrit roots: prati and ahar. Prati means "against", and ahar means "intake". In pratyahara, we stop searching externally for things to consume. By going within, by settling ourselves in the centre of our being, we defeat the desire for constant stimulation, for constant intake. We become so content that we just forget it.'

'How do we achieve this?' I asked.

'Something has to draw us inward,' said Daaji. 'This cannot be achieved by force. Otherwise, we end up struggling. You see, what often happens is that a person closes their eyes and tries to meditate, but they don't find anything inside. It is as if the heart is locked up—totally inaccessible. After a few minutes of trying, they are frustrated. "I don't feel anything!" they say. Then they give up. Or, they persevere and force themselves to concentrate on the heart. But then, they are not really meditating. It is only concentration, which is not the same thing.'

'Why don't we find anything when we look inside?' I asked.

'We haven't developed the inner senses that would allow us to perceive anything on that subtle level,' said Daaji. 'We are like a blind person attempting to recognize the colour red. Divinity is already within us, but we don't recognize it. We do not feel it. Therefore, it has no effect upon us.'

'How do we rise beyond this limitation?' I asked.

'In the Heartfulness approach, our meditation is aided by yogic transmission,' said Daaji. 'That makes all the difference. The topic of yogic transmission is a vast one, so let us wait and explore it in greater depth later on—including the way to experience it for ourselves. For now, let us understand that transmission is a catalyst for profound meditation. It allows us to experience Divinity—rather than only believing in it. By infusing us with divine experience, transmission helps us transcend the need for belief. When you experience something for yourself, belief is no longer relevant, you see. Therefore, transmission is a means by which we can awaken to reality, to the essential presence within. As a result, meditation now becomes a joyful, living affair. No longer is it just a dry exercise. No longer do we spend meditation fighting with thoughts and bodily sensations.

'Further on, yogic transmission helps us merge with that inner presence and become almost identical to it. You see, transmission is Divinity itself, coming to your door with an invitation in hand. Like the scent of a rose beckoning us toward the garden, the fragrance of Divinity draws us in. It is so mesmerizing and captivating! It speaks to our hearts and draws us further into itself—further into *ourselves*. This paves our way to deeper levels of meditation. It happens so naturally that we hardly have to expend any effort. That is why Babuji (the second guru in the Heartfulness tradition) called this Heartfulness path "the natural path", or Sahaj Marg. It is a natural and forceless approach.

'Now, having been drawn inward, we arrive at the sixth step in Patanjali's progression, which is dharana. Patanjali describes dharana as "arresting other things". This means that during meditation, you are undistracted. You will still hear the traffic noises coming from outside. You'll still be aware that someone is in the next room talking loudly on the phone. Yet you are unaffected by these inputs. They do not disturb you. Their impact is *arrested*.

'However, as a result of Patanjali's definition, people generally mistake dharana for a state of intense concentration. Let's examine its etymology. Dharana stems from the Sanskrit root dhar, which means "something that holds", or "something that contains". So, like a tiny fetus that is held and supported in its mother's womb, we are also held and supported. Where? In the womb of the heart. When we are totally at rest in the heart, something special happens—something sacred, actually. In nature, seeds germinate in the womb of Mother Earth because of the comfort they find there. In this comfort, they split open and shed their protective layer. Why? Because they sense the protection of the Earth surrounding them. When we experience that same level of comfort and protection in the womb of the heart, the divine seed starts to open, and from that seed, a new spiritual life gradually emerges. We now start to experience a completely new spectrum of consciousness.

'In this situation, we experience profound rest. We experience comfort beyond description. When we are so restful, can the mind still be restless? Can our emotions create havoc within us? Everything now settles down, and we become content.

'You see, we do not have to hold the object of meditation in our minds, as people so often believe. That would be very tiresome. Rather, the object of meditation holds *us*.

'Patanjali's next step is dhyana, which is "to hold the mind on one object". But when the mind is at rest, we don't need to hold it in place. It is already in place. It is simply balanced there.'

'So dharana and dhyana are really describing one and the same condition,' I said.

'That's right,' said Daaji. 'There is no difference between an undistracted mind and a settled mind. They are indistinguishable.

'And let us not mistake a restful mind for a sluggish mind. No, in this state, our awareness becomes dynamic. Consciousness steeps in the divine presence within. We are totally absorbed in it. When our level of absorption passes a certain threshold, we call it "samadhi", which is the eighth and final step in Patanjali's progression.

'Because samadhi is the last of these eight steps, people commonly think of it as the grand culmination of the spiritual journey. In actuality, samadhi is only the beginning. Much, much more lies beyond. Actually, many of us have a taste of samadhi even on our very first day of meditation, just as you did on yours. Our experience of samadhi deepens and changes as we progress, you see.

'Samadhi is deep meditation. It is to be deeply absorbed in the divine object. Then we start to unite with that divine presence within. Eventually, we become one. However, total union does not happen all at once. It is a progressive thing. You see, with each successive meditation, it can be possible to merge a little further. And along with each tiny union, we experience a sense of completion that is unmatched by anything we have previously experienced. Our hearts become drenched in peace and contentment. When such is the case, could anything possibly disturb us? Could we still feel stressed or unbalanced? *The mind is only at ease when the heart is at peace.*

'Yet, many regard meditation as a state of mere mental inactivity—of thoughtlessness. Not many have understood that the roots of inner stillness lie in that state of union. People often take mental stillness as a goal in and of itself, without realizing the *cause* of that stillness. Believing that meditation is an exercise in suppressing thoughts, they devise various artificial means to induce the state of thoughtlessness. There are certainly points on the body which, if concentrated upon, do provide thoughtlessness. (That is the reason that some people meditate on the tip of the nose.) However, thoughtlessness without union is only a state of ignorance—of mental dullness—and not of any use. That is not samadhi.

'Let us now examine the word itself. "Samadhi" is a combination of two Sanskrit roots that mean "equal" and "original". Sama means "equal", and aadi means "original". So in samadhi, we enter into a state that is equal to the original state, which is the state that prevailed before we came into existence. At that time, nothing yet existed apart from the Source from which we emerged. In that state, there was perfect calm and perfect balance.

'In fact, sama not only means "equal", as I just described, but it can also mean "balance".

Therefore, we can also translate samadhi as "original balance".'

'So samadhi is a state that is equal to our original state, which was a state of balance,' I said.

'Exactly,' said Daaji. 'There is even a third way to form the word "samadhi". Combine sama, meaning "balance", with the root aadhi, which means "mental disturbance". According to this combination, samadhi also means "balancing mental disturbance". This is a revealing description! In samadhi, the disturbed mind reverts to its original balanced nature. Balance is intrinsic to the mind. Disturbance is artificial. It came later on. It is something *we* created.'

'And we continue to create it,' I said.

'Yes,' said Daaji. 'Disturbance depends on our efforts, but balance doesn't depend on anything at all. When you leave things alone, they become balanced by themselves. A pond only gets ripples when something disturbs it. On its own, it is placid.'

'So we cannot create balance,' I said.

'And neither can we create samadhi,' Daaji replied. 'We meditate, and samadhi comes on its own. It is what remains after everything else has settled down. *This is meditation: effortless focus upon the infinite object.*

'With a limited object, your awareness is limited. Many people recite mantras, for instance. But by repeating a single word over and over again, they only straightjacket their minds. They confine their awareness to the narrow perimeter of the word they are repeating. Focusing on a limited idea, your awareness is single-pointed. When your awareness is single-pointed, you miss out on everything except for that single point. You are like a horse wearing blinders in that you see the object in front of you and nothing else. Your awareness is confined.'

'What happens when your object is *unlimited*?' I asked.

'With an unlimited object,' said Daaji, 'your exclusive awareness encompasses the limitless totality of existence. Everything is included in such an awareness. Nothing can escape it. But does this mean that you are simultaneously aware of each person in the world, of every dog and cow, of every particle in the universe? No! The awareness we gain in meditation is not an awareness of diversity in its various forms. Rather, it is of oneness. It is an awareness of the Whole, of the Totality. If the Whole has any quality at all, it is Being. It is pure presence, pure existence.'

'And we are also a part of That,' I said.

'Yes,' said Daaji. 'You cannot be separate from it. It is not as if you stand upon some mountaintop, gazing down at the infinite! Rather, you *become* it. Your situation now recalls the old Vedic pronouncement, *Tat Tvam Asi*: That Thou Art. And it is the truth! You are *That*. But you will not realize this.'

'Why not?' I asked.

'Because in the infinite, you have melted away,' said Daaji. 'You are no longer there. And if you are no longer there, who will perceive this truth? Now, the knower dissolves in knowing. The drop merges in the ocean.'

Daaji paused.

'But that is not the end. No, it is only a beginning…'

Attitude

One afternoon, I meditated alone with Daaji. Afterward, he remarked, 'Meditation isn't everything.'

'What do you mean?' I asked.

'Spiritual practice is important,' he said. 'Without it, transformation is only a dream. Yet, even the most effective meditation method, combined with the most disciplined approach, can only take us about 5 per cent of the way.'

'And the other 95 per cent?' I said.

'Attitude,' said Daaji. 'What we do is important,' he said, 'but it's not as important as the attitude with which we do it. This doesn't only apply to meditation. With any activity, it's our attitude that defines it and our attitude that determines its success. If you meditate in a negative mood, it is counterproductive. Your negativity becomes the object of your meditation, you see. Your eyes may be closed. You may look as if you're in meditation, but in actuality, you're just brooding over your negative thoughts and feelings. That becomes your focus. And what happens if you meditate on your bad mood?'

'It only intensifies,' I said.

'The purpose of meditation is to enter into the finest states of consciousness,' he continued. 'Do you think that will be possible if you bring heaviness, discord, and torments along with you? We have to leave them all behind. Such things weigh us down like lead, but they are easily removed with the cleaning method.

'There are also other attitudes that hinder us in subtler ways. Expectation is one of them. You see, many approach meditation with the expectation of a certain result. Suppose that one day, you had a phenomenal experience in meditation. The next time you meditate, you want to relive that experience. In so doing, you apply a condition to your meditation. "I *must* feel peaceful today!" Something better might be waiting for you, yet you only want peace. So you miss out.

'This shows how even the best experiences can become traps. We have the tendency to get stuck on our experiences. Rather, we should always be willing to go beyond, to go further. Even at the high stage where bliss finally dawns, you must keep moving. Otherwise, your desire to remain in that state of bliss holds you back. You like it so much that you want to repeat it again and again. You don't want to transcend it. Be assured that whatever you may experience, there is always something beyond it.

'We should also avoid the opposite extreme, which is impatience for the next stage to come. We needn't be in any rush to keep moving. This attitude also holds us back.'

'I guess it's a fine line between getting stuck on an experience and being in a hurry,' I said.

'No, not at all,' said Daaji. 'It's a simple thing.

Just let the process unfold naturally, with total openness. Don't place any conditions upon it. Don't insist on anything and don't demand anything. Meditation is best when we have no expectations—not even for meditative experience! If something happens, fine. If you have no experience, it's still okay.

'Really, meditation is a form of waiting. Not impatiently, as if you are pacing back and forth waiting for the bus. It's a relaxed kind of waiting. You are at ease. You are comfortable. It does no good to be impatient, you see. Everything happens in its own time. For example, you cannot cut open a butterfly's cocoon before it's fully matured. That would kill the butterfly. Similarly, we cannot expect spiritual states to bloom before their time. They will come!'

'Sometimes, we have unpleasant experiences,' I said. 'What then?'

'Many things happen in meditation,' said Daaji. 'But every experience is ultimately good because each experience has a purpose—even if we don't understand what it is. We need not understand it either. Our understanding is not necessary for us to keep moving. Just take your experiences lightly and move on. Most of us do not understand the intricacies of the spiritual journey. Even if we have a vague idea of the destination, we still don't know all the stages that come along the way. Stages are innumerable! Sometimes, the road appears to go backward. Sometimes, there is no road. Yet, we are moving forward in our journey through consciousness. So experiences can be deceptive. For instance, we previously spoke about samadhi.'

'Deep meditation,' I said.

'Yes,' said Daaji. 'But not every meditation ends in samadhi. Some days, there will be no depth. Some days, our meditative experience is too mundane for our liking. Then we worry that something has gone wrong. This shows our unfamiliarity with the path. In many cases, there is a good reason for an uncomfortable meditation. We go through periods of discomfort from time to time. The biggest reason is that we have taken a quantum leap in our journey—we have taken a big step forward. Some inner transformation has taken place, and we now have to get used to our new state.'

'What do you mean?' I asked.

'It's like moving into a new apartment,' said Daaji. 'You walk into a room and fumble for the light switch on the left side, but now it is on the right. It takes time to get used to your new surroundings. The best approach is to refrain from judging our meditative experiences and the states of being that they create in us. Instead, be like a passenger on a train, simply observing the passing scenery.

'On this journey, many scenes do pass by our window. We already spoke about how our experiences reflect our inner state, how our anger and ego give us bad experiences and how our kindness and humility give us blissful experiences. But there is a far deeper nature that we all share—a divine nature. That is our hidden nature. And it is a changeless nature, too. As we progress, our outer nature slowly evolves to match that changeless, innermost nature. Until we become identical with that changeless state, we have to undergo constant change. We have to move through so many conditions of being before we reach that fundamental state. All the while, we have experiences that reflect these inner changes. Change can be tumultuous because there is no stability in change. Even though these changes are positive and reflect more overall balance in our personality, they still take a little getting used to. And a certain amount of restlessness will continue to remain within us until we reach the changeless state.

'Somewhere along the way, in the midst of all our experiences, we stumble across the Source of all these experiences, the inner cause of our transformation. That moment is an important one. Your heart just melts in gratitude. You are so moved, you see. You fall in love with the inner Being.

'Now, your focus shifts. You no longer care about experiences. You no longer care about peace or happiness or any passing condition. Why do you want peace when you can have the Peace-Giver? You no longer care about transformation, either. Meditation now becomes an act of love—pure and simple. It's not about getting anything or experiencing anything—only love.

'This cannot be forced. It happens by itself, naturally. Often, you don't even notice that it has happened! Somewhere along the line, you fell in love without even realizing it. It's like a girl who realizes that she's been in love with her friend for years, without ever knowing it.

'And whenever there is love, longing is also present—the craving for togetherness. That craving contains a subtle pang. It is the pang of separation.

It's the lover's pain of being away from his beloved. This longing can become profound. This is the first stage of *bhakti*.'

'Please explain what bhakti is,' I said.

'It has many aspects,' said Daaji. 'The main one is the quality of devotion, meaning that you are lovingly devoted to the highest ideal. You are in love with the Divine. This cannot happen unless you have had some experience of the Divine. But even then, that experience only creates a craving for a more complete and permanent experience. It proves to you that there is something wondrous, something beyond the physical reality. Yet, having had such an experience, you then find yourself thrown back into the mundane. The experience has passed, and you no longer feel the divine presence so clearly, so tangibly. It was only a glimpse, so now you begin to crave it in earnest. As a result, you recommit yourself to your spiritual practice. You devote yourself to it. A new sense of purpose starts to drive you.'

'The pain of longing that you are describing seems to run counter to the attitude of non-expectation and openness that you discussed earlier,' I said. 'I mean, to crave and to be non-demanding seem like contradictory approaches.'

'It's the most beautiful contradiction,' said Daaji.

'But how does it work?' I said. 'How do you reconcile them?'

'I'll share an example,' said Daaji. 'There are some places in the world where if a boy wants to marry a girl, his family barters for her. If the girl's family still refuses, his family might even kidnap her. Compare that to a boy who gets down on one knee with flowers and a ring. "Darling, will you marry me?" he asks. With all his heart, he wants to marry her—*but he allows the choice to be hers.* His love is non-demanding. It surrenders to the object of its love.

'Longing is fine, but it should contain no force. It should be respectful. Reverential, even. And it should be accepting. Love never compels, you see.

'Without a craving heart, it is easy to be non-demanding. Would you be demanding about something that you don't even care about? It's only when you long for something with all your heart that the sentiment of non-expectation becomes noble. That is the second stage of bhakti. In the first stage, there was love and longing. In the second stage, there is still love and longing, but there is also a graceful acceptance of your situation, whatever it may be.

'Acceptance is a cheerful thing. There is no such thing as grudging acceptance. You are either grudging or you are accepting! You can't be both. Acceptance is from the heart. You cannot force yourself to accept a situation that your heart is rejecting from inside. In real acceptance, there is joy. Even if the girl you love says no, you are still happy. Love does not exist for the sake of receiving anything in return. That would be sacrilege. Rather, it exists for its own sake. You love for the sake of love. That is unconditional love, which is the only kind of love that there is. Love demands nothing. In love, there is no place for expectation, but only for gratitude. That is why love is the pinnacle of human nobility.

'When love backs our actions, we never feel resentment. We never feel put upon. We never feel life to be a chore. This is especially true with meditation. Our hearts should call out for it. Practising meditation should never be a matter of discipline or willpower. It's okay if you don't feel like meditating one day. It's natural. In that case, however, it is better not to do it. Suppose you tell your wife, "Darling, I am using all of my willpower to sit beside you." End of married life! No lover meets his beloved out of a sense of obligation. Think back to those days when you skipped school to meet a girlfriend. If she said, "I'll meet you at the movie theater at 11:00," you'd be there by 10:30. Perhaps she'd arrive by 10:00 just to test you! Some people regard meditation as a discipline, you see. They use willpower to get out of bed in the morning and meditate. Willpower is useless stuff. It means you don't have interest. When you really look forward to meditation, you wake up automatically. You don't even need to set an alarm. If you do set one, you'll wake up before it goes off. A joyful anticipation runs through your subconscious all night as you sleep and by morning, your heart is already dancing. You're in meditation even before you sit.

'Of course, we cannot expect this attitude at the beginning! It takes some time for it to develop. Rather, it takes time for it to become *conscious*. Bhakti is innate, you see, but it is unconscious at first. At some point, though, it surfaces to our conscious awareness. It becomes a sentiment, an emotion. But it cannot stay that way forever. It's like a whale that surfaces, just for a moment. It takes a breath and dives beneath the ocean waves again.'

'Why does it not remain a conscious feeling?' I asked.

'A love relationship consists of two,' he said, 'the lover and the beloved. However, when there are two, there is also separation. They are distinct from one another—separate entities. This is inherent in the term "bhakti". Bhakti is derived from the Sanskrit root, bhaj. The word has varied meanings, but one crucial meaning is "separate". Without separation, without the distinction of lover and beloved, there can be no relationship at all. But if lover and beloved remain distinct, love also remains an unfulfilled promise. There is no consummation—there is no *union*.

'Some people enjoy that state of longing. There is emotion in that longing. Perhaps they would prefer to stay there forever. However, we should not stay there. There is no utility in longing unless it leads to union. And in union, there can be no relationship either, *because there are no longer two*. Lover and beloved have now become one. That is the consummation of love.'

'So in relationship, there is no togetherness, and in togetherness, there is no relationship,' I said.

'It is a paradox!' said Daaji, with a laugh. 'When lover and beloved become one, they lose their individual identities. There is no longer any distinction between them. So tell me, when there is no lover, who loves? And when there is no beloved, who receives love?

'You see, love is something that never really arrives. We approach it, and before we arrive, we have already transcended it. But we never pass through it! It gets closer and closer, and when it can get no closer, the whole business is already behind us. It is a mysterious thing!

'That is the destination to which we ply on this journey. We call it union, but it is actually beyond union.'

'How is it beyond union?' I asked.

'Because union contains a subtle feeling that two have become one,' he said. 'But if there is any feeling of two, how can it be union? In real union—when two have truly become one—there is no idea or feeling of two. Hence, we never become aware that we have united with the beloved. We forget ourselves and the beloved, as well. This state is beyond union. "Yoga" means union, and so it is also beyond yoga.'

'But yoga is the path that takes us there,' I said.

'Yes,' said Daaji. 'And yoga is not a single path. It contains so many schools and philosophies. It is a hugely diverse system. Three of these paths are especially well trodden. They are *karma yoga, gyan yoga,* and *bhakti yoga*. Although they are thought to represent different paths of yoga, they are not at all separate from one another. They are actually three aspects of one single path. That single path is called *raja yoga*. Raja means "king", so raja yoga means "king of yogas". It incorporates the other three.

'We have started to explore the meaning of bhakti. Now, let's take a brief look at karma and gyan yoga. Karma means "action". It's a broad term. If we want to be literal, we can call each and every thing we do karma. Tying your shoelaces is karma. Eating a sandwich is karma. But those things are not karma yoga. Karma yoga is the yoga of action. It is the action we take in order to achieve the goal of yoga.

'There is an old saying: "No animal jumps into the mouth of the sleeping lion." In order to achieve, we have to act. We have to *do*. And why do something? The path of karma yoga has traditionally focused on developing the quality of desireless action—*nishkam karma,* as it is called. In nishkam karma, you are supposed to act without thinking of any result. But without a result in mind, why would you act at all? Action comes only when you have a particular goal in mind. Yoga has a well-defined goal, and this goal demands action.

It will not happen simply because you wish for it. Any action we undertake for the sake of attaining that goal now becomes karma yoga. Therefore, meditation is karma yoga.

'Now let's take a look at gyan yoga. Gyan means "knowledge", and so gyan yoga is the path of knowledge. But can it be enough to simply read books or philosophize? A rigorous intellectual process is not sufficient. By itself, it will not enable us to perceive ultimate reality. Only meditation can achieve this. With meditative practice, the mind becomes an unfiltered medium, allowing only truth to pass through it. Then our thinking no longer misleads us, but brings us to the right conclusions instead. Therefore, meditation is gyan yoga as well.

'Through meditation, we are also able to better understand the wisdom of others who have walked the path before us. Unless we meditate, such knowledge tends to go over our heads. It does not resonate with our experience, so we cannot relate to it. Often, a beginning meditator may read a spiritual book, but they may not understand much of it. If they read it again after having meditated for some time, they'll start to find gems that they didn't notice on the first read. Certain books—such as the books by Babuji—have so much depth that no matter how many times you read them, you'll always find something new. Even after four decades, his writings still reveal new things to me.'

'From what you're saying, it seems like meditation facilitates both approaches,' I said. 'It facilitates both gyan and karma.'

'It is the *essence* of both approaches,' said Daaji. 'It is through meditation that gyan and karma come to fruition. Bhakti also. So meditation is key. These three themes—karma, bhakti, and gyan—are universal. In every spiritual movement, at least one or two of these themes is present. They may not be called by their Sanskrit names, but they are there. We find the combination of gyan and bhakti in nearly every religion. For example, almost every religion contains a scriptural element. That is gyan, or knowledge. Religions also tend to have a devotional element, which is bhakti. But not every religion offers a practice that would allow an aspirant to experience the truth of its scriptures for themselves, and to have a real, non-imaginary experience of the object of their worship. In other words, even when gyan and bhakti are present, there isn't always a functional element of karma yoga. Of course, every religion has its own rituals, and in the widest sense, those rituals do represent action, or karma. After all, those rituals are actions taken by the seeker for the sake of coming closer to the deity. But in order to become conscious of the Divine, consciousness must first evolve to a divine level. Without a sound meditative practice that can accomplish this, the Divine will remain an abstraction to us.

'So, it is through practice that we gain knowledge—gyan—and it is through practice that we nourish bhakti. If you haven't come into real contact with the Ultimate Source, what kind of bhakti can there be? You haven't experienced anything. You haven't truly known the Divine. Without practice, bhakti remains disconnected from its object. It becomes externalized. We think of God, and our imaginations start working. Perhaps we imagine a glorious being, seated upon a heavenly throne. Or, we conceive of an abstract source of power and energy. God exists, but until we go within and feel that presence, God remains a concept—a mental formulation.

'With the imagination, you can create many things that are not real. In fact, you can only create things that are unreal. You may create wonderful illusions. You may create terrible hallucinations. They are your own creations, and they are unreal.

'Meditation does not create anything at all. Meditation reveals. What does it reveal? That which is real, that which is authentic, that which is true. Lies are created. Untruth is created. Reality can never be created—it is as it is.

'You see, meditation itself is bhakti. The word "bhakti" has become synonymous with worship in its various forms. To some, it is making offerings to God. For others, it may be singing devotional songs. These are outward expressions of love. But when such outward expressions are devoid of inner feeling, worship becomes mechanical. Then, it is only a ritual—all form and no essence. It is like an empty husk or a lifeless body. Yet, when that inner feeling—that attitude of bhakti—is indeed present, should any outward expression be necessary?

'That is why meditation is a silent activity. It is worship, but an *inner* worship. In deep meditation, worship is no longer an act, but a state of being, an intrinsic quality of the heart. This is only possible when the object of worship is internal.'

Daaji paused.

'Of course, this does not mean that you worship yourself!' he said with a laugh. 'That would only be vanity. Some would even call it blasphemy. Rather, it means that you come into an ever-deepening contact with the divine presence inside your own heart.

'The Divine is everywhere, but in that case, it is also within you. So why look externally? When the Divine is found within, we call it the Self with a capital *S*. We find it when we plunge into to the absolute depths of consciousness. There, you find that there is something upon which consciousness rests. You find that consciousness has a foundation. Then you go even deeper and find that that foundation has its own foundation, and that under this foundation is an infinite foundation. This infinite foundation is the Self, the underlying reality of all things, animate or otherwise. Yet, it has no existence of its own. It is beyond existence and nonexistence, you see. Nevertheless, it is the root of all existence. It is its support. *And then there is something beyond that, too.* But by realizing the foundation of universality in your own heart, you transcend all that is individual, all that is limited.

'However, the term "Self" can be deeply misleading. When we read or hear the word, it can conjure up a feeling of "I-ness", or individuality. Yet, the yogic concept of Self implies something universal. It is the common Self, a Self that is both impersonal and deeply personal. It is the heart and soul of each and every thing.'

'If the term is so easily misunderstood, why use it?' I asked.

'Often, I don't,' said Daaji, 'for this very reason. At the same time, it also shows us something important. It shows us that it is impossible to find that universal foundation outside of oneself. To find it, you must go within. By going to the foundation of your own existence, you discover that shared foundation, the common denominator for all existence. Thus, it is through the personal that you discover the universal. It is through the subjective that you realize the objective.'

'How do you know when you have encountered the Self?' I asked.

'You cannot know,' he replied. 'To find the Self is to forget yourself entirely. You cannot be conscious of having found it. If you are, then you haven't found the real Self. Then, it's only your ego. Real meditation begins when you are no longer aware that you are meditating. It begins when you go beyond experience.'

'But you have been speaking so much about how we must experience the Divine, rather than just thinking about it or believing in it,' I said.

'Yes,' said Daaji, 'but truly speaking, we never experience the Divine, but only the *effect* that it has upon us. The divine Self does not act upon us, but because of it, we are transformed. The Self does not inspire us, but through it, we become inspired. The Self does not bestow anything upon us. It has nothing to give. But because of it, we receive. We must go beyond all this. To meditate for the sake of receiving anything is against etiquette. The best attitude is one of love and gratitude, which develops over time as a result of our ever-deepening contact with the Source within. Again, I say that yogic transmission brings this about very quickly. As a result, meditation becomes the true essence of worship.

'Such worship is devoid of any pomp or show. It is devoid of words, forms, and even ideas. Simply put, it is to melt away in that loving essence. Then, two become one, and even the idea of worship falls away. That is bhakti at its highest pitch, and it comes through the practice of meditation.

'Of course,' Daaji added, 'we also find many examples of meditation practices that do not lead to bhakti. I would call that mechanical practice. It's a technical approach, having no heart, but only discipline.

'So, as I said earlier, all three approaches are necessary—karma, bhakti, and gyan. They are three legs of the same stool. Remove any one of them, and it becomes nonfunctional. But combine the three together, and the result is greater than the sum of its parts. It's superb. Raja yoga combines the three, with the effect that we are immediately put into contact with the Self. This happens in our very first meditation session. There is one very old text, *Amanaska Yoga* by Gorakshanatha, which describes the Self as a king seated within us.'

'And raja means "king", I said.

'That is why this path is called raja yoga,' said Daaji.

'And that is what Heartfulness is,' I said.

'Yes,' said Daaji. 'It is a streamlined version of raja yoga—streamlined in the sense that it has been made effective for modern seekers who don't have the luxury of dropping everything and devoting every waking moment to meditation.'

'Regarding all these approaches to yoga that you have just described, which should be our main focus?' I asked.

'Focus on the practice,' said Daaji. 'Focus on the three elements of the Heartfulness practice: meditation, cleaning, and prayer. Practise them meticulously. Practice is the most important thing because it is through practice that everything else comes. Without practice, there is no karma, bhakti, or gyan. Without practice, there is no yoga. It is practice that leads to mastery of yoga, and mastery of yoga only means mastery of one's own self. That is what a master is—one who has mastered themselves. As Babuji said, "I have not come to make disciples. I have come to make masters." So practise.

'However,' he added, 'it is yogic transmission that makes the practice of Heartfulness so transformative. Like the fabled philosopher's stone that turns even lead into gold, transmission can ultimately transform even the hardest heart into a sacred temple of God.'

Yogic Transmission

As a new meditator, I was mystified by the concept of yogic transmission. Initially, my intellect rejected the idea because it was beyond the scope of anything I had ever heard of or even considered plausible. On the other hand, my own experience of transmission was that it was the best thing that had ever happened to me. Therefore, I struggled to bridge my worldview with my own experience. But experience has a funny way of changing a person's worldview. Having already meditated for a few years without transmission, I could clearly perceive that the two experiences were fundamentally different from one another. With transmission, meditation gained a new dynamism. More importantly, it became transformative. I immediately noticed profound changes in myself, which continued to unfold over years. When I became a Heartfulness trainer, I learned how to help others meditate with transmission as well. Yet, transmission remains mysterious—as all sacred things must be. Therefore, I was eager to hear what Daaji would reveal about it.

'Yogic transmission is the hallmark of our method,' said Daaji. 'On its own, our meditation technique is just another technique—no better or worse than any other. But transmission is absolutely unique. It is what makes *all* the difference. Transmission is the key to the Heartfulness approach. It's what makes this method so powerful.'

'In many spiritual traditions,' I said, 'the term "transmission" refers to the means by which a teaching is conveyed. However, its meaning is different here, in the Heartfulness context.'

'Divine knowledge is never *taught*,' said Daaji. 'Rather, it is *caught*. It is absorbed by the sincere seeker when the moment is just right. In the field of spirituality, teaching becomes a paradox. Until you become awakened, any teaching will fall upon deaf ears. After awakening, teaching becomes unnecessary. Real awakening does not come from hearing inspired words. Nor does it come from reading books. It cannot. No description of a spiritually awakened state can create that same state in another, no matter how eloquent it may be. Between guru and aspirant, there is a resonance of hearts. The awakened state is transmitted like a flame passed from one candle to the other. The guru triggers that resonance and through it, creates a state of spiritual awakening in the student.'

'What is transmission exactly?' I asked.

'In the mundane world, we are already familiar with the concept of transmission,' said Daaji. 'For instance, we can transmit sound, we can transmit speech, and we transmit so many other things as well. With yogic transmission, we transmit the very essence of spirituality. Transmission is a sacred emanation from the Original Source. It is nothing less than this. We could call it the essence of God, and that would also be correct.'

'So transmission doesn't originate from the person transmitting,' I said.

'Does a fan create the air that it blows on

you?' he replied. 'We are surrounded by air at all times, but we don't notice it unless there is a breeze. In the same way, we tend not to notice the constant presence of Divinity in our lives, though it surrounds us and infuses us. However, with transmission, that presence becomes subtly animated. The divine energy moves. It moves toward us and moves within us. Like leaves dancing in the wind, our hearts begin to vibrate along with that divine flow.'

'What role does the guru have in this?' I asked.

'The guru is like a ceiling fan,' said Daaji. 'His role is to trigger that movement. Transmission doesn't belong to him. He doesn't own it. Nobody does! Transmission is the essence of nature. In Sanskrit, we call it "*pranahuti*". Let's examine this word. Pranahuti comes from two root words: prana and ahuti. Classically, prana means "life force", but people generally understand prana as "breath". This understanding may be correct if you view it as the breath of the Ultimate.'

He paused.

'You see, transmission utilizes prana's subtlest essence,' he said. 'We could go even further and call transmission the *essence of the essence*. Its subtlety defies expression. It is equal only to Divinity.

'However, a question now arises. Do we not

already have that essence within us? There is already an entity within that provides us with that continuous impulse of existence.'

'The soul,' I said.

Daaji nodded. 'You know,' he said, 'in India, the summer is very hot. The land becomes parched, and the leaves on the trees start to die. In fact, the whole tree looks as if it is about to die! Yet, its roots absorb just enough moisture and nutrients from the Earth to keep it alive. But when the monsoon rains finally arrive, the trees really come to life. They even look as if they are dancing! They have so much freshness. They are so vibrant.

'Just as a tree draws moisture and nutrients through its root system, we continuously draw sustenance from the soul. But when we receive our very first dose of transmission, we become like a tree dancing in the monsoon rains. Our lives gain a new freshness—an unimaginable freshness! In a very real sense, new life is breathed into us.

'Now we come to pranahuti's other Sanskrit root: ahuti. Ahuti means "offering". It can also be taken to mean sacrifice. Remembering that prana is the essential, elemental life force, we now understand that transmission, or pranahuti, is an *offering* of that pure essence.

'To whom is this offering made? It is made to

us. The Ultimate Source offers itself to each of us. In this light, we are reminded of Christianity, where the Lord sacrifices himself for the sake of all, where he gives of himself. So, we can understand transmission as a process by which the Ultimate infuses us with its own essence. As a result, our job becomes easier. We do not need to trek into the jungles as so many spiritual seekers have done throughout the ages. We do not have to ascend any steep mountains. As the saying goes: "If the mountain will not come to Mohammed, then Mohammed must go to the mountain." Since time immemorial, aspirants have been going to the mountain. They have suffered there. They have made sacrifices. They have taken great pains and made great renunciations for the sake of the Divine. But with transmission, it is the Ultimate that makes the sacrifice. The mountain *does* come to you. This becomes the impetus for an extraordinary spiritual expansion.'

'How so?' I asked.

'When a higher force acts upon us, we need not rely upon our own limited capacities,' said Daaji. 'Just think of the oxygen tank worn by a scuba diver. It allows her to breathe underwater, which normally she could not do. This enables her to dive deeper in the ocean and remain submerged for longer periods of time. Similarly, transmission enables us to access levels of consciousness that could normally take years or even decades to achieve on our own. There are also certain passes that are nearly impossible to access. Transmission keeps us moving through all of them.

'Some stages of the spiritual journey can be extremely attractive to the seeker. They are filled with such joy, peace, and bliss. In fact, they are so compelling that we become tempted to settle down there and abandon the spiritual journey altogether. But this would be like staying in the same school class, year after year. There would be no evolution. Sadly, many seekers lose their way like this. Transmission will never allow for this, however.

'Some stages are so wondrous that we think there's nothing more to achieve. *I made it!* we think. But there is always something more. It is an infinite journey, after all. In an infinite journey, the path itself becomes the goal. It is to put one foot in front of the other and continue evolving. Transmission provides us with that evolutionary pull. It literally plucks us out of one stage and deposits us in the next, at just the right moment. In that sense, it acts as safeguard, preventing stagnation at any stage of the journey. Otherwise, we could remain in certain places for a very long time. In fact, we could remain there forever.'

'Forever?' I said.

'You see, every stage can be infinite,' said Daaji. 'In mathematics, for instance, you can have a line that has no beginning and no end. It stretches to infinity in both directions. But is it actual infinity? It's only a line. It is one-dimensional. In a similar way, it is possible to expand infinitely in a sort of one-dimensional fashion. That is what happens when we stop moving, when we are satisfied with whatever we have already achieved.'

'What effect would stagnation have on us?' I asked.

'You would become imbalanced,' said Daaji. 'Just as every country has its own customs, every stage along the spiritual journey has its own characteristics. It has its own essential quality. The longer we stay at any juncture, the more we absorb its essential quality into ourselves. It is good to stay in a stage for some time and absorb its essence, but only to a certain extent. If we were to stay there too long, our growth would become lopsided, so to speak. It would be like going to school and learning only one subject. What use is it if you can do astrophysics but don't know how to read? So even when we stagnate, we are still growing. But in that case, we are only growing in one dimension, in one direction. It is not a holistic growth. It is not evolutionary, but extreme.'

'So transmission prevents this from happening,' I said.

'Yes,' said Daaji. 'It keeps us moving under all circumstances. It also accelerates our journey. Without transmission, you would have to work extremely hard and for a very long time in order to move from one stage to the next. That is why the spiritual journey is traditionally thought to be so long and arduous. In the mythological lore of India, you find stories of people meditating for thousands of years! If you believed those stories, would you feel like starting the journey? Yet, many do. Spiritual history is replete with tales of sincere aspirants who retreat to forests, caves, and mountaintops, where they put themselves through extreme austerities—all for the sake of spiritual illumination. In India, it is widely accepted that one must undergo hardship in order to attain the highest states.

'I once thought the same. As a teenager, I was

inspired by Ramakrishna Paramahansa and his disciple Swami Vivekananda. In the late nineteenth century, Swami Vivekananda traversed the entire country of India—largely on foot—spreading his inspiring message wherever he went. Well, in May 1976, when I was nineteen years old, I decided to follow in Vivekananda's footsteps and left home to be a wandering monk—a *sanyasi*, as we call them in India. But unlike Vivekananda, I had no message. I was still searching for spiritual awakening. I was purely a seeker.

'On the banks of the river Narmada in Gujarat, I encountered a band of sanyasis on the veranda of an old temple. I knew nothing about their way of life. I noticed an old man with matted hair, who seemed to be their leader. His life of austerities had made him thin and frail. Eventually, he called me and asked what I was doing there. I told him that I sought something beyond what the world could promise.

'You will find God,' he said, 'but not like this!'

'This old sanyasi was straightforward and sincere. He poured his heart out to me, in fact. He was filled with regret for taking this path in life. He told me how he had left his home as a young man. He hadn't informed anyone. Nobody knew what happened to him. He just disappeared.

'I never saw my family again,' he said. 'My wife…I don't know what happened to her. I don't know what became of my children.'

'He was haunted by all this. He had also become disillusioned with his path. After years of wandering and begging for alms, his spiritual goal still eluded him. His search was genuine, but misdirected, you see. And he knew he had gone the wrong way. In fact, he had considered returning home decades earlier, but couldn't face his family.

'I can still hear his parting words: "You will not find God like this!"

'How long did you live like this?' I asked.

'About six hours.'

Hearing this, I burst into laughter. I had assumed that Daaji had spent weeks, or even months, wandering around rural India.

'When did you first experience transmission?' I asked.

'On 12 August 1976,' said Daaji. 'At the time, I was living in a hostel at my pharmacy college. Sometimes, I would try to meditate, but I didn't really know how to do it. I would sit on my bed and try to think profound thoughts. One of my fellow students observed me doing this over a period of time and said, "Hey Kamlesh, why don't you let me take you to someone who can teach you how to meditate properly." He put it very crudely, actually. "I know a chick that can put you in a trance," he said. When he took me to meet her, the "chick" turned out to be an elderly woman! And the "trance"? It was samadhi, the eighth step in Patanjali's *Yoga Sutras*. Often, people think samadhi to be an extremely high attainment that takes many years to achieve. But with transmission, it came immediately.

'I remember how warmly this woman welcomed me when I arrived at her home. When she asked why I had come, I related my earlier experience with the sanyasis. She said, "It is true that God is in the jungles and mountains where those monks roam. The Divine is everywhere. *But if God is everywhere, He is also inside you.* In that case, why seek Him in any other place?"

'I was struck by this statement. She invited me to meditate along with her, and in this meditation, I received transmission for the first time. That experience just finished me off! Never before had I experienced anything like it. I was so impressed. Then, she impressed me again. After the meditation was finished, she had tears in her eyes. She was so grateful that I had come to meet her. Imagine the trainer being grateful to the student! It occurred to me that I had never witnessed such humility before. I had the same thought all over again when I first met Babuji, who was her guru as well.

'Now, how could a novice like myself have been able to have this kind of experience in the very first meditation? It was due only to transmission. Without transmission, we struggle to master even our everyday, mundane consciousness. I have met many seasoned meditators who still have difficulty with meditation, even after years of practice. My wish for them is that they experience transmission at least once in their lives. That is what allows us to transcend the mundane consciousness. Our consciousness gets an upgrade, you see. It becomes divinized.'

Then Daaji laughed. 'Of course, now you have to learn to handle your divinized consciousness. That's another story!'

He paused.

'We also use transmission to create noble qualities in the seeker. Here, I'm reminded of Patanjali's *Yoga Sutras* again. The second of his eight steps is called niyama. Lalaji [the first guru in the Heartfulness tradition] had an interesting take on niyama. He defined it as "the infusion of noble qualities". This is exactly what we accomplish with transmission.

'And while we're talking about the *Yoga Sutras*, it also bears mention that transmission helps us fulfill its fourth step as well.'

'Pranayama,' I said.

'You see, most people think that pranayama is only a set of breathing exercises,' said Daaji. 'That's why the word "prana" is usually associated with the breath. But pranayama has a deeper meaning. The word is composed of two roots: prana and aayaama. We already discussed the traditional meaning of prana, which is life force. Aayaama means "expanding".'

'So "pranayama" means 'expanding life force",' I said.

'Right,' said Daaji. 'It has nothing to do with breathing, per se. Whenever we receive transmission, we are receiving the very highest force into our hearts. From there, it expands throughout the entire system. "Expanding life force." So this is how yogic transmission fulfills the objective of pranayama.'

'And this is the reason that breathing exercises are not part of Heartfulness practice,' I said.

'Yes, when we have access to transmission, pranayama becomes redundant,' said Daaji. 'But that doesn't mean that transmission and pranayama are equivalent to one another.'

'I've read that Ramakrishna transmitted his spiritual wealth to Swami Vivekananda,' I said.

'Yes,' said Daaji. 'It's true. Swami Vivekananda was also able to transmit, but never spoke about it. There are other examples to be found as well. Transmission is present in certain strands of Sufism, for instance. There, it is known as *tavajjoh*. There is mention of it in Tibetan Buddhism as well, and there are also references to it in certain yogic texts, such as *Yoga Vasishta*. You see, transmission does not belong exclusively to any one path, just as God does not belong to any particular religion. If a person is completely merged in the Source, they can distill that divine essence and distribute it to others.

'But it is extremely rare to find such a person. Great personalities such as my gurus have hardly existed throughout history. You see, if a guru is not completely merged in the original Source, they still may be able to transmit. But in that case, what are they transmitting? Only their own, limited state of being. Such a person is not connected to anything higher than themselves. And even if they are connected to something higher, their transmission will be limited to the extent that they have not dissolved themselves in God.'

'And that limitation will inhibit the transmission's effectiveness,' I said.

'Of course,' said Daaji. 'You see, in the deepest levels of samadhi, our state resembles the original state that prevailed before we came into being. At that time, there was no movement, but only stillness. But in that stillness, there was immense potential. There was immense energy. When that energy is set into motion, we recognize it as the original force, or *adi shakti*. Yogic transmission is that original force. It is the adi shakti. Only the original force can bring us to the original state.

'In fact, an even better term than "original force" would be "forceless force". You see, transmission has an effect, but causes no reaction. Usually, force creates a reaction, but has no effect. When you berate someone, they react. But is there an effect? Does that intense scolding change them? Force always creates reactions. Only love can create an effect without causing a reaction. Due to transmission—this loving, forceless force—we are able to regain our original state of union with the Source, which is the very definition of yoga.'

'So in order to reach the ultimate state, the

transmission we receive must come from that ultimate level,' I said.

'Yes,' said Daaji, 'and only a person who has evolved to become identical to that ultimate state will be able to activate the Source, in the form of yogic transmission. Here, Lalaji made a key innovation. He discovered a method by which a person who is completely merged in the Source can prepare others so that they become vehicles, or conduits, for his own transmission. This discovery is what allows us to have so many thousands of volunteer Heartfulness trainers around the world, each imparting transmission on the guru's behalf.'

'So Heartfulness trainers are conduits for the guru's transmission,' I said.

'Yes,' said Daaji. 'The guru prepares them and works through them. A trainer can even be a novice meditator, but their transmission still equals that of the person who prepared them, who enabled them to impart transmission.

'In my view, this is a remarkable step in the history of spirituality because a mere beginner can now do the very same spiritual work as an evolved personality. And the guru is also a conduit in this process because really, it is nature's process! The guru is also a pawn, you see. Transmission is an aspect of nature's evolutionary work with humanity.'

'But in that case, shouldn't we receive transmission automatically, without having to meditate?' I asked.

'A farmer must prepare his fields if he is to be benefitted by the rain,' Daaji replied. 'Nature is as it is, so we attune ourselves to it. That is why we practise.'

'By which means is the divine impulse transmitted into our hearts?' I asked.

'What do you mean?' asked Daaji.

'Take sound, for instance,' I said. 'Sound requires a medium that can vibrate, such as air or water. Does transmission require any kind of medium in order to reach us?'

'In *Yoga Vasishta,* it is said: "By means of sight, by means of word, by means of touch, the one who can infuse Divinity in the disciple and enlighten him is indeed the real guru," said Daaji. 'In many yogic stories, we hear of situations in which a guru merely glances at a disciple, thereby awakening them. In the Sufi tradition, it is common for a sheikh to gently touch the chest of an aspirant in order to infuse their heart with spiritual energy. But in our way, we do not use any of these methods. We do not use physical touch. We don't need a guru or a trainer to look at us, and we don't need them to speak to us. Here, transmission flows unseen—but it is not unfelt! Its medium is thought. You see, the trainer merely thinks of transmission, and it begins to flow. But at times, it flows automatically, without the trainer even thinking about it. In that case, what would its medium be? Anyway, something only requires a medium if it has to travel somewhere. But transmission reaches its target instantaneously. Even light cannot travel instantly. If transmission can traverse any distance in zero time, its velocity must be infinite. That is because it comes directly from the infinite Source, which is in all places at once without being in any place in particular.'

Seekers start the Heartfulness practice by meditating along with a Heartfulness trainer, also known as a *preceptor,* who triggers the transmission on their behalf. These meditation sessions are called *sittings*. Sittings can take place in-person, or they can happen remotely, where the trainer and aspirant meditate at the same time in different locations.

The role of the trainer does not end after the initial sittings. Rather, trainers continue to be available for ongoing sittings. Ideally, the aspirant takes a few sittings per month from a trainer. The main purpose of taking ongoing sittings with trainers is to provide us with opportunities to receive transmission. This supplements our daily individual practice. Our daily practice also helps us digest and absorb the transmission we receive during sittings.

Trainers are not selected because of their degree of advancement. They are chosen based on their willingness to serve and their knowledge of the Heartfulness approach. They need not be any more advanced than the seekers they are serving. They are volunteers performing a certain service, and just like any other aspirant, trainers must practise daily and take regular sittings from other trainers.

'I would say that to have so many trainers who are endowed with the capacity of transmission is unprecedented in the history of spirituality,' said Daaji. 'In the past, transmission was hidden. It was a completely esoteric art. Now, it is freely available.

That it remained hidden in previous times is not due to the selfishness of those who had the capacity to transmit. It's just that today's paradigm is different. Humanity's evolutionary stage is different. The times now demand that transmission be widespread. That is where Heartfulness fits in, its role being to fulfill this need. To serve all is its *raison d'être.*

'Spiritual service must be selfless. We could never think of charging for transmission. That would be sacrilege. Babuji used to say that he received all that he got for free, so he freely gave all that he had. God is not for sale. He has no price. If He did—and if you could afford to pay it—then why would you need Him? If anybody ever asks you to pay for spiritual service, ask them that question.

'My dream is for all spiritual movements to unite together and benefit from this transmission. I always say that there is no need for you to leave your religious or spiritual tradition. Transmission is for all of humanity, you see. Regardless of your religion or culture, you can meditate with transmission. It does not matter whether you are Christian or Muslim, Jewish or Buddhist—transmission will only enhance your faith. You see, faith is the result of our experiences, and transmission is the giver of experience.

'However, no matter how highly we may speak of transmission, it can only be truly appreciated through direct personal experience. Words will never capture its essence. The attempt to grasp transmission intellectually is like trying to intellectually understand the taste of a peach. Is it possible to convey the experience of eating a peach to someone who has never tried one? You can describe its shape, colour, texture, and scent, but until you eat one, you won't know anything about it.

'Therefore, I suggest adopting a scientific approach and testing transmission for yourself. Create an experiment around it.

'For example, in pharmaceutical research trials, volunteers are divided into two groups. The researchers administer the real drug to one group, while administering a placebo to another study group, which is designated as the control group. This process enables the researchers to evaluate the effectiveness of the new drug against the placebo.

'In our experiment, meditation without transmission is the placebo, or the control. By meditating without transmission, we experience the effects of meditation on its own. The next step in the experiment is to connect with a Heartfulness trainer and meditate while receiving yogic transmission. Having meditated first without transmission and then with transmission, we become able to compare the two experiences.

'You see, I do not want people to take my word for anything that I have said about transmission. Try it for yourself and arrive at your own conclusions.'

PART TWO

Practising Heartfulness

3

Meditation

IN THE HEARTFULNESS way, we sit comfortably every day at a fixed time and place, and meditate on the presence of divine light in the heart. For me, meditation is a daily source of clarity, lightness, inspiration, and palpable inner joy. Even though I have meditated in this manner nearly every day for fifteen years, my discussions with Daaji opened new dimensions in my understanding, and yielded profound advances in my practice.

When and Where to Meditate

When I first started Heartfulness, I meditated whenever and wherever I wanted. At that time, I attached no significance to the time or place of meditation. Later on, when my life became more hectic, I started scheduling meditation into my day. The differences between meditating at random times versus meditating at a fixed hour were striking. Shortly thereafter, I had to move my meditation to the early morning hours. Then, my meditative practice really took off!

Now, years later, I hoped that Daaji would explain the reasons behind these experiences.

'What is the best time for meditation?' I asked.

'Now,' he said.

'Okay, but are certain times better than others?' I asked.

'Is there a bad time for meditation?' he replied. 'You know, I'm reluctant to make any pronouncements on this matter. I don't want to create any dogma on the subject. To do so would deprive people of the joy that comes with discovering the truth on their own.'

'I understand that,' I said, 'but I think that we could benefit from knowing some best practices.'

'Okay boss,' he said with a laugh. 'Well, our elders have passed down so much wisdom regarding meditation timings. But I am a practical person, so I say that you should meditate at the time when you are the least likely to be disturbed! In this busy world, it may not always be possible to meditate at the most ideal time, you see. There are numerous household activities—raising children, going to work, et cetera. So many demands are present, so we have to choose our time carefully. One solution is to meditate early in the morning, when there aren't so many things competing for your time and attention. But if you like it, you'll do it no matter what.

'You see, a sincere meditator will never say, "Oh, it's not convenient for me to meditate today." Suppose you tell your friend, "I'll only meet you when it's convenient for me." That means that your convenience is more important to you than your friendship. Meditation is another kind of meeting. It's a sacred meeting with the Self, which is our friend within.'

'But still, people are so busy these days,' I said. 'Many tell me that they have no time for meditation.'

'I'm reminded of one incident,' said Daaji. 'Once, a senior minister in the Indian government came to meet Babuji. This official was interested in meditation, but said that he had no time for it. Babuji responded by asking him whether anyone was busier than he.'

"Yes," said the official. "The Prime Minister is

busier." At that time, the Prime Minister was Indira Gandhi.

'Babuji replied, "Then give me the difference between her busyness and your busyness and devote *that* time to meditation."

'If meditation had really been a priority, he would not have complained about how busy he was. He would have simply made the time. By contrast, the woman who taught me to meditate was immensely passionate about meditation. She faced a lot of opposition from her family, though. Intense opposition! So how did she handle it? Every day, she woke up before everyone else and meditated in bed while pretending to be asleep. Sometimes, she pretended to use the bathroom and meditated there. Her life revolved around meditation, you see. If you're passionate about something, you will always find a way. As the saying goes, "Love laughs at locksmiths."

'Busy people should also understand that meditation provides many shortcuts in life. Often, we invest a lot of time and energy in various endeavours. Sometimes they come to fruition, and other times they do not. For example, someone courts a romantic interest for years, but eventually, the other person backs off. Or, you may expend a lot of time trying to build a business relationship, but it proves fruitless in the end. Wouldn't it have been better to understand the reality of these situations from the very start? Meditation provides a level of insight that allows us to appreciate situations for what they actually are. This can save us years of time.

'Therefore, meditation is an enormous timesaver. I would even say that the less time you have, the more vital meditation becomes. If you can meditate for even five minutes at a fixed time every day, it will be of great benefit. So do meditate—*especially* when you don't have enough time!'

'So you recommend meditating at a fixed time,' I said.

'See, we have to create automatism in our practice. That means that we should meditate at the same time and same place, daily—whatever that time may be. This must become second nature. It should be so automatic that we never have to think about it.'

'Why is this regularity so important?' I asked.

'See how nature is,' said Daaji. 'It has unfailing rhythm. The sun rises and sets, the seasons turn, the tides rise and recede. All this happens with absolute precision, with absolute rhythm, with total regularity. Our lives are also governed by nature's rhythms. When we are in tune with them, we sail through life. Otherwise, it is like swimming upstream. We struggle.

'Take sleep cycles, for instance. If you go to bed at the same time every night, you'll be asleep as soon as your head hits the pillow. You won't ever have problems trying to fall asleep. Similarly, if you meditate at the same time every day, meditation will happen by itself. It will happen so naturally. You won't ever have to expend effort in order to meditate deeply.

'Our forerunners also discovered that certain times in the day are especially conducive to meditation. They referred to these times as *sandhyas,* or "conjunctions". They call them conjunctions because these times are moments when one part of the day joins another. At such moments, nature is supposed to attain a state of balance. By meditating during these periods of balance, we absorb that balance into ourselves. It becomes part of our nature, you see. These junctions are the hour before sunrise, noon, and dusk. For me, noon is the best. It just works like a rocket!'

'Do you mean solar noon or noon according to the clock?' I asked.

'I mean noon!' said Daaji, with a laugh.

'For me, meditation is so much better before sunrise,' I said.

'This is why I encourage people to test these timings for themselves,' he said. 'Meditate before sunrise. Meditate at noon. Is there a difference? Now, compare that to the effect of meditating at a completely different time. You have to find what's best for *you*.

'Do not be too rigid with any of this. For instance, how will you meditate at dawn if you live above the arctic circle, where night lasts for six months, and the day lasts for another six months? Or even in parts of Scandinavia, where the sun rises so early and sets very late? The most important thing is regularity. To meditate at one of these recommended times is ideal, but it is of secondary importance compared to our regularity in meditation.

'And it is just as important to have a fixed place for meditation as it is to have a fixed time. For instance, when you enter the kitchen, you think about food. Even if you're not hungry, you're tempted to grab a snack. So what happens if you dedicate one room for meditation? By the time you sit in your meditation spot, you're almost meditating already. If on the other hand you meditate in a different place every day, you'll spend time trying to get comfortable. The newness of your environment will distract you, even in subtle ways. As a result, you won't be able to meditate as deeply as you might otherwise.

'Further, our thoughts, emotions, and activities leave traces in the atmosphere. When entering any place, we resonate with what we feel there. For instance, if you visit a hospital, you'll immediately notice certain effects. You'll feel some lingering sadness. You'll feel heaviness around you. There is worry floating in the air.

'Many years ago, I wanted to open a new pharmacy in New York City. One of my employees scouted a great location. It was right next to a hospital. (That's generally a good spot for a pharmacy.) The owner was willing to sell it, too, and for a low price. I was almost ready to buy it sight unseen. But I went to see it, and as soon as I entered, I felt that something was wrong. At some point during the tour, I went to use the restroom. The moment I entered that room, I felt such a disturbance in the atmosphere. There was a certain helplessness, an immense sadness. I felt that there was a spirit hovering in that area, and I just turned around and left. But even as I walked out, I was haunted by what I can only describe as a cry for help. Later, I asked my employee to find out what had happened there. It turned out that it had recently been the scene of a murder.

'The effects of thoughts and actions linger in a place. By meditating again and again in one place, we create a special atmosphere there—a meditative atmosphere. Peace and sanctity pervade such an atmosphere. It is light, subtle, and pure. In fact, it becomes a holy place. At the same time, all places are holy! Every atmosphere is divine—until we corrupt it with our thoughts, emotions, and activities. That is why we should avoid performing other activities in the place where we meditate.'

'Not everyone can reserve an entire room in their house for meditation,' I said.

'You can even dedicate one corner for the purpose,' he replied, 'like cats that always nap in the same spot.'

'In the same way that there are ideal times for meditation, are there also ideal places?' I asked.

'Choose circumstances that do not interfere with your practice,' he said. 'For instance, you don't want an environment that is filled with distractions. When your environment is chaotic, your consciousness reflects that disorder. Inner disturbance tends to intensify in the presence of outer chaos. When you sit in a cluttered or dirty room, it affects you. If clothes are scattered everywhere, if books are lying open and dirty dishes are stacked up in the sink, how well can you meditate? A spare, open environment is best. Ideally, your meditation space should have only the chair or mat where you sit. Our external circumstances should be conducive to meditation, bearing in mind that meditation is an *inner* activity. There should be nothing in our environment to draw us outward, you see. But as we progress, we also develop the ability to be unaffected by our surroundings. For example, in the beginning, we tend to become angry if something disturbs our meditation. With time, external distractions only drive us deeper into ourselves.

'And of course, time and place are not the only two variables that can affect our meditation. On a daily basis, we expose ourselves to so many influences. These influences affect our mood. "Why do I feel low today?" It could be some interaction between your circumstances, your encounters, a dream you had, something you ate, a state of health. After a chaotic day, you cannot help but be affected. If you come home and meditate at that time, your meditation may not be as easy as if you had meditated first thing in the morning, for example. In the early morning, nothing has had a chance to affect you yet. You're a blank slate.

'So I hope people test all these things for themselves. Meditate before eating. Meditate after eating. Do you find a difference? Meditate before bathing. Meditate after bathing. Is there a different effect? People have spoken and written much about these topics. Some say that we should meditate only after bathing. Well, what about meditating after splashing just a little water on your face? Is that sufficient? So try these things and see for yourself. You'll come to the correct conclusions.'

The Meditative Posture

Before I encountered Heartfulness meditation, I experimented with a few other meditation methods. Whatever their differences may have been, they all shared one commonality. Each attached great importance to posture. In those early days of my meditative journey, I had the impression that profound meditation would only come once I had mastered the meditative pose. As a result, I devoted a lot of energy and attention to my posture. I also looked forward to the day that the pose would become second nature and I would never have to think about it again.

Before one of my early meditation sittings from a Heartfulness trainer, I asked which pose I should adopt. She looked at me and said, 'Be comfortable!' I was a little surprised. A short time later, I met some of the local meditators practising Heartfulness. There, I was surprised again. Among the group, I found no strict adherence to any one particular pose. Many people sat cross-legged. Others sat in chairs. Nobody looked rigid. Everyone sat in a way that was natural to them. Since then, I have rarely heard Heartfulness meditators even speak about the subject of posture. So, I decided to bring it up with Daaji.

'What is the ideal meditative pose?' I asked.

'We have to look at posture in the context of meditation's larger purpose,' he said.

'What do we do in meditation? We go within. We move toward the core of our being. In deep meditation, we come into contact with our Source. Dissolving in it, mingling in it, and merging in it, we become one with it. This union represents the true state of yoga. It is a return to the Source from which we originated. Thus, yoga represents the principle of dissolution. It is a return to the moment before our creation, when everything was converged into a singularity. In that singularity, there was no activity. That is why the state of yoga is a state of perfect calm and inner stillness.

'In life, we also find another, opposing movement. It is that which pulls you outward, away from your core. This outward movement represents the principle of creation, which is an active principle.

'However, we must understand that the moment of creation is also a moment of *separation*. It is the moment that we become separated from our Source. For instance, what happens when a mother gives birth to her baby? It's a creative act, but it is also a moment of separation. Previously, mother and baby were one. When the mother ate, the baby ate. Their existences were intertwined. After the baby's birth, they became two distinct entities. One became two.

'Similarly, the creation of the soul is the moment that it becomes separate from its Source. For the first time, unity is lost. For the first time, we experience incompleteness. We experience dissatisfaction. Certain theologies call this "the fall". With meditation, we re-enter that state of unity and stillness. We regain our originality, our universality.

'Many people believe that we can only return to the Source after death. Then, there is the voice of logic, which tells us that the only way we could return to the Source would be to go back in time! Neither is true. Through meditation, we achieve that grand union here and now, while still alive. To master yoga is to transcend the limitations of death and the limitations of time. In the state of yoga, we simultaneously express the principles of creation and dissolution. We are beyond that duality. We are simultaneously active and inactive, time-bound and eternal.

'This comes with deep meditation. You may wonder what posture has to do with any of this! But the state of deep meditation begins with posture. Our meditative pose can help us turn inward and move us toward our centre. Or, it can get in the way.

'We've already discussed several of the eight steps of Patanjali's *Yoga Sutras.* The last four steps—pratyahara, dharana, dhyana, and samadhi—illustrate our plunge into deep meditation. From pratyahara, which is to turn inward, we proceed through dharana and dhyana, where we rest in the heart. Finally, we enter samadhi, when we start to dissolve into the Source.

'Patanjali's third step is asana, which means "posture". In order to choose the best asana, we should consider which pose will best lead to pratyahara, dharana, dhyana, and samadhi. The first thing we do in meditation is to turn ourselves inward. That's pratyahara. Our physicality can help us here. If our eyes are wide open, if our bodies are sprawled out, and if our legs are stretched in front of us, it's not going to help us to go within. Such poses lend themselves to a more external orientation. To achieve pratyahara, our physicality has to adopt a contracted form.

'This is, of course, a matter for personal experience. So try both ways. Meditate with your arms and legs stretched out. Meditate with them folded. Then see the difference for yourself.'

'I've already experimented with this,' I said.

'What did you find?' he asked.

'It's just as you said. It was harder for me to really go inside when my limbs were stretched out.'

'That's why the traditional posture for meditation is a seated pose with folded legs,' said Daaji. 'The position of the hands is also important. Ideally, they should be clasped together with the fingers interlocked. Or, you can rest one hand on top of the other. And we meditate with closed eyes.'

'In some methods, people meditate with open eyes,' I said.

'The ancient literature describes the senses as the gates through which awareness flows,' said Daaji. 'Sight is the most prominent sense. We tend to focus upon whatever we see, so closing that gate of sight helps us reorient our awareness inward, which is pratyahara. From asana and pratyahara, we then proceed through the rest of the steps: dharana, dhyana, and samadhi.

'In samadhi, we enter into a state of union with the Source. From the Source, we draw a subtle current of energy. By sitting with folded limbs, we form a kind of circuit. This circuit allows that current to flow throughout our system. It passes from limb to limb, cycling around and around again. If our limbs are not in contact with one another, that circuit is broken, and the current escapes and goes to waste.'

'If the Source is infinite, what does it matter if a little energy goes to waste?' I asked.

'You know,' said Daaji, 'I once had a personal discussion with Chariji [the third guru in the Heartfulness tradition]. He said, "Kamlesh, make as much money as you like. Go ahead. But spend it wisely!" Chariji's statement contained a hidden question, you see: *If you spend your money wisely, then why would you need so much of it?* When you truly value a resource, you want to make the very most of it. You conserve it. In meditation, what we receive is the very highest. It's the divine essence! So I think that we would not want it to go to waste. The truest form of gratitude is to make good use of what you receive. Posture may seem like a small thing, but in this respect, it cements our relationship with the Source.

'But don't worry if you can't sit with folded legs. It's okay. In that case, sit on a chair with your feet on the ground. But cross your feet at the ankles—one over the other. That allows you to retain some of the cross-legged effect. If you have bad knees, then don't try it. You can just keep a small mat under your feet, instead. This will help prevent energy drainage, as long as it's made from non-conductive material.'

'This idea is completely new to me,' I said.

'The ancients tended to meditate on animal skins,' said Daaji. 'It's because skin is non-conductive. But other materials are just as good. You can sit on a woolen cloth, or a silk-covered cloth, if that's more comfortable. A wooden plank, a carpet, or a cushion will all work.'

'What about a sofa?' I asked.

'Yes, a sofa or chair will also suffice,' he said. 'As long as the material is non-conductive, it's okay.'

'Is it alright to use some kind of back support when we meditate?' I asked.

'Yes,' said Daaji. 'Many people sit like that and meditate well. But we should definitely avoid resting the head when we meditate. That will put you right to sleep. For the same reason, we should avoid lying down when we meditate.

'However, if you suffer from insomnia, that is also the cure. Lie in bed and start meditating. You'll fall asleep straight away!

'Now, we have yet to discuss what I consider to be the most important aspect of posture. Your pose should not get in the way. If your pose distracts you from meditation, it defeats its purpose. I've just told you that the cross-legged pose is ideal, but is it ideal for *you*? Each body is unique. Some people prefer to sit on the floor, while others can't sit without a chair. Because there is such difference between bodies, we can never expect uniformity. We can never expect all people to adopt the same posture for meditation. The cross-legged pose works well for some, but other people can't meditate like that. If a pose doesn't work for you, then you should not force yourself to adopt it. It is like the Hippocratic Oath: "First, do no harm." In fact, Patanjali seems to say the very same thing: *Sthira sukham asanam*. "Posture should be steady and comfortable."

'Patanjali does not insist that we sit in full lotus position. Nor does he say that we should sit on the ground. He only says, "Be steady and comfortable." Why should we be steady? If you're constantly changing your position and fidgeting around, you won't be able to meditate. Physical steadiness is necessary.

'Now, how to achieve this steadiness? There are two ways. The first way is to be forceful. That is not recommended, of course! Yet, with great effort, it is surely possible to ignore your body's pain signals and force yourself to be still. Of course, everything will hurt, and you may even injure yourself. But you will be as steady as a rock. Will your mind be as steady? Most likely, it will be busy with the body's sensations of pain and discomfort. Then, that becomes your object of meditation. With this approach, you go against the body, while preventing the mind from meditating.

'When can both mind and body be steady? Only when you are comfortable. That is the second way—Patanjali's way. Without comfort, you fidget. You shift your position this way and that. Continuously, you search for comfort. Then there is no steadiness. When you are comfortable, on the other hand, you have no reason to move. The body does not want to move. You are just fine where you are. Then the body does not distract you.

'We should also avoid excessive comfort. That also binds our attention to the body. Now, it is not as if we are against the body. In fact, we really must thank the body because it is the jumping board from which we dive deeper into consciousness. But we have to jump, and not cling to the board, so for that reason, we avoid any extremes that will make us focus too much on the body. "Moderation" should be our watchword. Therefore, we avoid both discomfort and extreme comfort during meditation.

'Now we come to Patanjali's next verse: *Prayatna saithilyananta samapattibhyam.* "By relaxation of effort and meditation on the endless, posture is mastered."

'Let's understand this. What does it mean to master something? When something is mastered, it becomes second nature. We don't have to think about it. We don't have to expend efforts for it. To be masterful is to be effortless, you see. If you have to expend efforts to achieve your pose, you have not mastered it, and until you have mastered it, you are its slave. So let us not meditate in difficult positions that require so much energy and attention. That only distracts us from meditation. When we are comfortable in our pose, we can turn our attention to the real object of meditation, which Patanjali refers to as "the endless".

'In the samadhi state, you plunge so deeply inside yourself that you lose bodily awareness. Then your head droops. Your body may even slump forward. You have forgotten the body, and in this forgetting, you have transcended it. Only then can we say that the pose is truly mastered. But this has to happen naturally.'

'So we don't slump on purpose,' I said.

'That would be artificial,' said Daaji. 'Rather, you should start meditation in an upright pose, relaxed and comfortable. As you go deeper into meditation, you'll lose awareness of your pose, and that's fine. After all, this is meditation—not gymnastics!'

Relaxation

The relaxation method supplements the three core practices of Heartfulness. Compared to those practices, the method is a recent addition. Furthermore, the relaxation method is not strictly a spiritual practice, as its main purpose is to relax the body. However, physical relaxation also provides us with mental and emotional calmness, which facilitates deeper meditation. For this reason, we often use the relaxation method just prior to meditation. The method can also be used on its own as a simple stress-relief tool, according to our preference.

I vividly remember my introduction to the relaxation method. While sitting with Daaji in his office, he turned to me and said, 'Let me show you how to relax.' He proceeded to guide me through the steps of the method, pausing shortly between each one to allow its effects to settle.

When he finished speaking, I found such stillness within myself that I didn't want to move a single muscle. I didn't feel like opening my eyes. I didn't even feel like having a single thought. In fact, my state of relaxation was so profound that it was as if I was already meditating.

Now, one year later, we discussed why he added the relaxation method to the Heartfulness practice.

'I think that relaxation came more easily in early times,' he said. 'Our lifestyle was different then. These days, we have to consciously relax ourselves. See what a state we have come to. Now, we have to make efforts to achieve effortlessness!

'Effortlessness is essential to meditation. But instead, we tend to apply both physical and mental efforts. As we sit in meditation, we constantly adjust ourselves. We adjust our bodies, we adjust our thoughts, and we adjust our awareness. We make repeated attempts to rest our unsettled consciousness. In all this movement, can we possibly derive rest?'

'It only makes us further unsettled,' I said. 'The search for stillness ends up creating its opposite.'

'Then, we become tense,' said Daaji. 'We become stressed. I can tell you to be effortless. I can tell you to be open, to be undemanding, to be non-insistent. And you agree. "Yes," you say. "I will not expend any efforts in meditation. I will not seek anything; I will not demand anything." But what happens when you actually meditate?'

He let the question linger for some time.

'There was once a little boy who lived in the

foothills of the Himalayas,' he said. 'One morning, he woke up and saw a yogi flying in the sky. The little boy was impressed. The more he thought about this flying yogi, the more he wanted to be able to fly like him. He decided to track him down. He packed a small bag and left early in the morning. After asking around and taking a few wrong turns, some villagers directed him to the hut of this man. "I want to fly like you," said the boy.

'The yogi said, "Okay, why not? I will teach you, but for this, you will have to stay with me for many years as my servant. On the first full moon of your fifteenth year, I will teach you the method."

'So the boy stayed with him. He carried water from the well, gathered firewood, and cooked all the yogi's meals, but none of this hard work bothered him at all. He was too excited that he would soon be able to fly.

'Eventually, that day came. Filled with joy, the teenager bounded into his guru's room. "Tonight is the full-moon night, my boss. Please tell me how to fly." "Sure, I will help you," said the yogi. "Tonight, meditate at midnight, but whatever may happen, don't think of monkeys. They may jump in your mind, they may dance, they may try to attack you, but don't think of them. Then the teaching will come to you."

'So the boy said, "Oh, it's very simple, I can do this—no monkeys."

'At midnight, he sat on top of the roof and closed his eyes. First thing, a monkey came into his mind! *I am not supposed to think of monkeys!* he thought. He tried not to think of them, but the monkeys kept coming. All night long, he fought with monkeys. In the morning, he went back to the yogi and said, "This method is rubbish. You shouldn't have told me anything about monkeys!"

'You see, the boy lost his dream of flying because he was so focused on not thinking about monkeys. By trying not to think about them, monkeys came instead of the teaching. Trying not to do something is counterproductive. And even if you somehow are able to consciously drop your efforts, you still make subliminal efforts. You make unconscious efforts. You cannot help yourself! Effort is difficult to stop, you see. To enforce a state of effortlessness upon yourself requires the biggest possible effort you can make. It's counterproductive.'

'Why are we so effortful by nature?' I asked.

'Effort is rooted in our primal state of restlessness,' said Daaji. 'It is based on the soul's inherent need to return to its original state, to unite with the Source. That is what this restlessness really is, you see, and that is also what turns us into spiritual seekers. In all this restlessness, you are searching for something. You try to escape the dissatisfaction and unsettledness that you feel in the present moment. Furthermore, you hope that the next moment will bring contentment and peace. Meanwhile, you are afraid of repeating your past—a past that only led you to your present state of unsettledness. In all of this, you miss out on the endless possibilities of the present moment. Calmness eludes you. Inspiration eludes you.

'You see, we only drop our efforts when we become content. But we are only content when we finally drop our efforts!'

'So it's a paradox,' I said.

'It's a catch-22,' said Daaji. 'In the mundane world, we are accustomed to making efforts in order to attain a certain result. In fact, no result comes without effort. A hungry person can only drop their search for food once they have eaten. Fasting will not fill their stomach. In spirituality, however, different laws apply. In spirituality, the act of dropping your hunger is the only thing that feeds you. The true state emerges when we have dropped everything, including our search, our efforts, and our own selves. Then, the Self manifests in its transcendental beauty—the real beauty. In dropping your search, you become open to that which you seek. In dropping yourself, you become the very thing that you seek.'

Daaji paused. 'Of course, to abandon all effort doesn't mean that you stop meditating!' he said. 'Meditate more and more, in fact. Dropping your search only means that you drop your searching attitude in meditation. You drop your effortful, insistent approach. Action is necessary in order to achieve anything.'

'And action is the key element in karma yoga,' I said.

'Yes,' said Daaji. 'So we must meditate. We must practise. We must act. But our actions should be effortless. They should flow with ease.

'True effortless action only arises when we have been transformed from the inside out. On its own, the relaxation method cannot achieve this. However, the mental stillness that it produces triggers a greater receptivity to the divine impulse that is truly responsible for our transformation. You see, when we are filled with tension and worries, we tend to deflect the higher help that comes through transmission. By relaxing ourselves, we accrue greater benefit.'

'So the relaxation method is a kind of lubricant, which allows the real spiritual work to flow unhindered,' I said.

'Exactly,' said Daaji. 'The purpose of relaxing the body prior to meditation is only to facilitate that divine work. When we are in a deeply relaxed state, our interference in the process is minimized, and we become more receptive. We become open to the subtle showers of transmission that soothe our meditative hearts.'

The relaxation method consists of a set of sequential suggestions that help us relax. It is best when used immediately prior to meditation, but we can use it whenever we feel the need. You can also help others to relax by reciting the suggestions to them, as Daaji did for me. There is no need to memorize these suggestions verbatim. By understanding the essence of the relaxation method, your own words may intuitively emerge. After some time, you won't even require the method. You won't need to go through the entire process in such a systematic way. Within the space of a single breath, you will be able to relax yourself completely.

RELAXATION

- Close your eyes very softly and very gently.
- Let's begin with the toes. Wiggle your toes. Now feel them relax.
- Relax your ankles and feet. Feel the energy from Mother Earth entering the soles of your feet. Feel it move up your feet to your knees, relaxing the legs.
- Relax your thighs. The energy moves up your legs ... relaxing them.
- Now, deeply relax your hips ... stomach ... and waist.
- Relax your back. From the top to the bottom, the entire back is relaxed.
- Relax your chest ... and shoulders. Feel your shoulders simply melting away.
- Relax your upper arms. Relax each muscle in your forearms ... your hands ... right up to your fingertips.
- Relax your neck muscles. Move your

awareness up to your face. Relax your jaw ... mouth ... nose ... eyes and eyelids ... earlobes ... facial muscles ... forehead ... all the way to the top of your head.

- Feel how your whole body is now completely relaxed. Scan from top to toe—if any part of the body needs your attention, revisit it and ensure that it is relaxed.
- Move your attention to your heart. Rest there for a little while... Feel immersed in the love and light in your heart.
- Remain still and quiet, and slowly become absorbed in yourself.
- Remain absorbed for as long as you want, until you feel ready to come out.

How to Meditate

Having fixed a time and place and found a comfortable pose, we are now ready to meditate. We gently close our eyes and centre our awareness in the heart, supposing that divine light is present therein and that it is attracting us inward.

'What does it mean to suppose that divine light is present in the heart?' I asked.

'It is a hypothesis,' said Daaji. 'At first, we don't know what is inside the heart. We are waiting to find out. Meditation is an experiment in which we test this hypothesis that divine light is present in our hearts. The proof of this experiment comes when we actually experience it, through feeling.'

'How do we conduct this meditative experiment?' I asked.

'We relax and gently allow our awareness to rest in the heart,' said Daaji. 'Divine light is not a thought, but a feeling. This feeling cannot be manufactured. Therefore, we should not make attempts to think about it or to feel it. Meditation is really a form of waiting—relaxed, patient waiting, without any expectation. Therefore, we do not repeatedly remind ourselves that "divine light is present in my heart, and it is attracting me inward." We don't need to keep refreshing this idea. It's not a mantra that we repeat: "Divine light is in my heart, divine light is in my heart." That would only disturb us. It would be artificial and effortful. Rather, the thought of divine light must disappear from our minds in order to give way to the actual *experience* of light in the heart. The object of meditation is something that we feel, not something to think about.'

'But the definition of meditation is to think continuously about one thing,' I said.

'Yes,' said Daaji. 'And we are continuously and totally attentive to this idea, but it is a deeper attentiveness—a nearly subconscious attentiveness. People tend to misunderstand this. If you try to hold it as a conscious thought, you are only concentrating. That is not meditation.'

'What triggers this deeper attentiveness?' I asked.

'Your intention to meditate,' said Daaji. 'That is sufficient. You see, consciousness is vast. Most of it lies beyond our conscious awareness. The portion of consciousness of which we are aware is only a minute fraction of its totality. The thought of divine light pervades those deeper realms of consciousness that are beyond our awareness. So you do not need to wrangle with the thought of divine light at any conscious level. Even if this thought never occurs to your conscious mind, rest assured that you are still meditating.'

'So what do we actually *do* in meditation?' I asked.

'Simply relax into your heart-centered awareness and wait,' Daaji repeated.

'This method is almost too simple,' I said.

'Reality is simple!' he replied. 'And to achieve a simple thing, we must adopt simple means. Babuji used to say that it's easier to pick up a needle with your fingers than with a crane!'

'If only I'd known how simple meditation is back when I first started,' I said.

'But you learned through experience,' he said. 'That is the best way.'

'When I started, I was at a total loss as to how to handle this idea of divine light in the heart,' I said. 'Whenever I asked questions, people would just tell me not to think so much! So most of the time, I just ignored the idea of divine light. And even without this thought, I still went deep into meditation. But on some days, I would think, *Okay, today I'm really going to meditate properly. I'm going to think of divine light continuously.* Those days, there was no meditation at all! It was only struggle.'

'The concept of divine light is extremely subtle,' said Daaji. 'Babuji called it "light without luminosity". Now, this definition contains a big hint! At first glance, it can make us scratch our heads. Isn't luminosity the defining characteristic of light? Yet, by removing luminosity from the picture, we learn something vital. We learn that divine light cannot be visualized or imagined in any way. It cannot be electric light. It cannot be candlelight. It cannot be daylight, neon light, or light from any material source. It is not something that we can see. So what is it? It is something that we *feel*.

'That is why we involve the heart in this process. The heart is the organ of feeling, after all. The attempt to think about divine light tends to get in the way of feeling it. It keeps us tied to the mental plane and prevents us from going deeper.

'So, we have to take this thought in a very subtle manner. At most, we gently remind ourselves that divine light is present in the heart and that it is attracting us inward, toward the Source. We do this once, in the beginning. And, in fact, even that much is unnecessary. It is such a natural process. Everything happens by itself, you see.'

'Why not simply meditate on the Source?' I asked. 'Why even bring divine light into this?'

'How would you conceive of the Source?' Daaji replied.

I had no answer.

'The Source is infinite,' he said. 'It defies thought. It even defies unconscious thought. No matter how you conceive of it, it won't be the real thing.

'Divine light, on the other hand, is graspable. It may be subtle, but at least we can experience it. We can feel it in our hearts. This subtle feeling pulls us further inward. It takes us beyond light, actually, and delivers us at the Source itself.'

'So the reason we meditate on divine light is that we cannot meditate directly upon the Source,' I said.

'Exactly,' said Daaji. 'But that light comes from the Source, and it draws us toward the Source as well. In this process of approaching the Source, we go deeper and deeper into meditation. We achieve greater and greater depths of samadhi.'

'But let's back up for a second,' I said. 'It isn't always the case that we close our eyes and immediately plunge into samadhi. Often, there's a lapse of time in between. That is when people experience the most difficulty because they have to contend with so many distracting thoughts. So my question is: How should we handle our thoughts?'

'Yes, thoughts are the number one complaint,' he chuckled. 'But to come with the expectation that "I must have a thoughtless state" is a wrong approach. We get carried away by these popular notions. Just as the ears are for hearing and the eyes are for seeing, the natural function of the mind is to think. When you're absorbed in a film that you're watching, you are not disturbed by your thoughts. But that doesn't mean that you don't have thoughts.'

'You're just inattentive to them,' I said.

'Right,' said Daaji, 'because you are more attentive to the activity that you are witnessing on the screen. The same thing happens in meditation. When we are more attentive to the heart than to our thoughts, they no longer bother us. This becomes easier when you start to feel the presence of the light within. You may not be aware that what you are feeling is the divine light. You may hardly even notice when it comes, in the same way that you don't notice the moment that you fall asleep. It just happens. Then, you're no longer affected by thoughts.

'Thoughts and emotions are like waves on the surface of the ocean. They may disturb the sailor who stays upon the surface, but not the whale, which swims in the depths. In deep meditation, we sink into those depths. Even when a gale blows, it remains above the surface, and we remain unaffected.'

'But what do we do before we sink into deep meditation?' I asked again. 'How do we handle our thoughts then?'

'Accept them,' he said. 'Love them, even. Thoughts are not your enemies. If you fight with thoughts, you will surely lose! The more you fight with your thoughts, the stronger they become. In fact, we can bring in Newton's third law here. In the physical dimension, every action produces an equal and opposite reaction. On the mental plane, that rule applies in an unpredictable way. There is still an opposite reaction, but it isn't equal. It is disproportionate! It's like throwing a stone into the ocean and getting a tsunami in return. So don't fight with your thoughts. Just let them be.

'Of course, that doesn't mean that you should indulge them, either. Often, we get pumped up by certain thoughts that impress us. We also get worried by our negative thoughts. Thinking is okay, but indulgence is never good. Really, thoughts should be like the wallpaper in a room. You may appreciate the beautiful print, or you may dislike it, but either way, it doesn't obsess you. It doesn't prevent you from carrying on with your activities.

In the same way, your thoughts need not hinder your meditation.'

'But sometimes, thoughts seem to ambush us,' I said. 'Then, it's difficult to stay poised.'

'Babuji pointed out that when you pour wine from a bottle, it leaves from the same opening from which it entered,' said Daaji. 'The thoughts we have in meditation are like wine flowing out of its bottle. They have been inside us all along, even if we weren't aware of their presence. We only become aware of them when we're meditating and they start coming out. Thoughts come only to leave, you see. So let them come.

'Sometimes, we experience really intense thoughts and emotions during meditation. They can be unsettling. The reason is that we tend to repress such thoughts and feelings in the normal course of our lives. You have thoughts that you think are bad, and you say, "No, no, no!" and push them down into the recesses of your subconscious. That doesn't get rid of them, though. They remain inside you, shading your experience and shaping your behaviour in subtle ways. In meditation, such thoughts resurface. They are like the air bubbles that rush upward in a pot of boiling water. Know that they are in the process of leaving you and pay them no mind.

'I am always happy when someone complains of a turbulent meditation because it shows that they have released something that they were harbouring inside. So, I think that we should refrain from judging our meditative experiences. What is far more significant is the way that you feel *after* your meditation is complete—not during. It is meditation's long-term effects that we are really after.'

'But how to handle a difficult experience in meditation?' I asked. 'Like when your thoughts just run away with you.'

'Just remind yourself that you are meditating,' said Daaji. 'That should be enough. If that doesn't help, then open your eyes for thirty seconds or so. That will clear the condition. Then you can continue your meditation.

'A time also comes when we do enter into a thoughtless state. This happens when we go further into the subtler realms of consciousness. The great Swami Vivekananda once said, "Consciousness is a mere film between two oceans, the subconscious and the superconscious" (Vivekananda: 2009). Let's look at these two words: sub and super. By pairing the prefix "sub" with the word "conscious", we see that the subconscious is beneath our conscious awareness. Conversely, the superconscious is above our conscious awareness. So the sub- and superconscious are both beyond our conscious awareness. Yet, one is a lower unconsciousness, while the other is higher.

'The subconscious is vast, as is the superconscious. In fact, both are infinite. With yogic practice, our conscious awareness expands through both of them. When we sleep at night, we dive deep into oceans of the subconscious. Actually, this occurs through a special state of yogic sleep called *yoganidra.* We'll discuss this later when we take up the subject of prayer. It is also necessary to purify the subconscious. It is filled with the remnants of past experiences. It's also the home of our lower instincts and drives. We'll also go into this subject more deeply when we discuss the cleaning method.

'Now, let's discuss the superconscious. It is the godly realm, and in meditation, we soar into its endless skies. It is from there that wisdom descends. It is from there that inspiration strikes your heart. In the superconscious, we are suffused with energy from the Source.

'In meditation, our awareness expands through the superconscious. At first, we may not have any experience of this at all. It is as if we are in a state of deep sleep. That is the first stage of samadhi. But slowly, we become familiar with the superconscious. We become aware in that state, and gradually, we gain command over it. Then, is it still superconsciousness?'

'What do you mean?' I asked.

'When you are conscious of it, it's no longer *above* your conscious awareness. It has become your normal state of consciousness. The superconscious is something that is always beyond. It is what you cannot access. What may be a normal state of conscious awareness for you may be a state of superconsciousness for someone else.'

'So it's a relative term,' I said.

'Yes,' he replied. 'We can also accelerate this process of moving into the superconscious state by using two supplemental practices called point A meditation and point B cleaning. But these practices are best explained in person by a Heartfulness trainer, after we have become established in the essential Heartfulness practices.

'In our journey, we also move beyond superconsciousness. In fact, we move beyond consciousness altogether. Consciousness is infinite, whether we are speaking of the subconscious or the superconscious. But that infinity is supported by another infinity, which we call *potentiality*.'

Daaji stood up and disappeared into his bedroom. A minute later, he returned with a book in hand: *Efficacy of Raja Yoga,* written by Babuji in 1944. Daaji started to read:

> Consciousness is not our goal. It is only a toy for children to play with. We have to reach a point where consciousness assumes its true form (i.e., what it really ought to be). We have to make a search for the mother tincture from which medicines are actually prepared. We are searching for the potentiality which creates consciousness, and if that too is gone then we find ourselves on the verge of true Reality, pure and simple. This philosophy is too high to be described adequately in words (Chandra: 2009).

Daaji closed the book. 'And Reality is another infinity that supports potentiality,' he said. 'You see, our development covers a spectrum that moves toward infinite subtlety. We begin with consciousness, move toward its potentiality, and eventually emerge into Reality. And we must go beyond that too...'

How Long to Meditate

Before I began Heartfulness, I used to meditate for precisely twenty minutes at a time. I would set an alarm and sit with closed eyes until it rang. Perhaps I learned this from a meditation class that I had taken, where the instructor would ring a bell when meditation was over.

When I started practising Heartfulness, I continued my habit of setting an alarm for twenty minutes. However, that 'ring' soon started to disturb me because it would come while I was still immersed in meditation. So, I started setting the timer for one hour instead. But then, I found that I would naturally come out of meditation exactly five minutes before the bell would ring. Soon, it occurred to me that the timer was only interfering in the process, and I never used it again.

I told Daaji about these early experiences, and he said, 'Yes, it's too artificial to set any time limit in advance. In fact, we should never set any agenda in meditation. We shouldn't impose any conditions at all. We have to be open, in a state of wonder and unknowingness.

'Sometimes we might think, *I have to go to work soon, so I'll just meditate for fifteen minutes.* The Giver knows your time constraints very well. Perhaps, he would have finished your meditation in thirty seconds, but you're insisting on fifteen minutes.'

'But in that case, I'm being more generous than the Giver,' I said. 'He needs thirty seconds, but I am allowing him fifteen minutes.'

'Maybe,' said Daaji, 'but what do you think will happen in those fifteen minutes? Instead of meditating on the endless, you will meditate on time, on limitation. You will be constantly aware that you have to stand up in a few minutes. You're focusing on the quantity of meditation—not the quality! If there is no quality, is there any use in quantity?'

'Sometimes when I meditate, I find that it's over very quickly,' I said. 'At other times, I find that an entire hour has gone by. What makes meditation complete?'

'It is complete when you have hit a satisfactory depth of consciousness,' said Daaji. 'Babuji recommended one hour. When people complained, he reduced it to half an hour. But he said that an hour was best. He had observed that people often take that long to reach a satisfactory depth in meditation.

'But don't run with this idea and say, "Okay, now I am going to meditate for one hour!" In that case, you'll still be meditating on the idea of time, and not on divine light. So forget time! Just meditate.'

'I've been told that Babuji never meditated for more than a minute or two at a time,' I said.

'He could instantly plunge into his inner depths,' said Daaji. 'If that's all the time you require, it's sufficient. And if it takes you one hour, that's also good.'

'What if you don't achieve any depth at all?' I said. 'Even in one hour.'

'Save it for next time,' said Daaji. 'So it didn't happen today. Fine. Try again tomorrow. Or, if you are really avid and you have some extra time, meditate a second time. But give yourself a little break. Take fifteen minutes, at least. Without this fifteen-minute break, meditation will create a slight negative effect.'

'What determines how quickly we can dive deep into ourselves?' I asked.

'It depends on the orientation of your awareness and the flexibility of your consciousness,' he said. 'Imagine that consciousness is a big circle. Its centre is the core of your being, the Ultimate Source. The circumference represents our surface-level awareness. It's our normal state of consciousness in which we interact with the world via the senses.

'Usually, our attention is unidirectional. It moves in one direction at a time. In meditation, it moves inward to the core. In our daily activities, it tends to move outward and away from the centre. It flows through the senses in the direction of the circumference.

'If your consciousness is nimble and flexible, it can easily switch directions. But if your consciousness is cumbersome, it's like a big cargo ship that requires four tugboats just to turn around. When we are accustomed to an external orientation, we tend to find it difficult to turn our awareness inward. Then, meditation takes a little longer. But with daily practice—and with the help of transmission—we develop a nimble consciousness, a flexible consciousness. Now, we can move in either direction, at will.

'However, as we develop even further, consciousness stops jumping back and forth, turning inward and outward. It stops being unidirectional. Rather, it expands in both directions at once. You are aware of what is happening around you externally. At the same time, you are moving toward the Source within. Furthermore, you are aware of what is happening in between the two. You have neither an inner nor an outer orientation.

Your consciousness is expansive. Your attention is inclusive.

'When this is the case, meditation no longer involves any movement. You're simultaneously immersed in the Centre—the Source—and aware of the external. That means that you don't have to turn your consciousness inward in order to meditate. In fact, meditation now becomes redundant. You are in a permanent state of meditation, you see. Why would you need to sit and meditate when you are already in meditation?

'You may have noticed that in Eastern iconography, spiritual figures are often portrayed in a meditative pose. We see this especially in depictions of Lord Buddha. He is always seated, always serene. In reality, though, illumined individuals do not sit in continuous meditation. They are active and engaged with life. One could be a busy emergency room doctor, for instance, busily attending to patient after patient. Despite her stressful situation, she is calm. She is peaceful. Her permanent contact with the Source provides her with an inner silence that pervades the surrounding noise. Despite her stressful circumstances, she is in meditation, you see. She may not be seated like a buddha figurine, but her consciousness is *buddha-*

like. She has attained permanence in meditation. This is called the meditative state.

'It should not be necessary to continue this daily exercise of meditation for your entire life. Each case is different, of course, but I think that if we still require this daily ritual after twenty or thirty years, something must be wrong in our approach.'

'So why are evolved individuals always portrayed in that meditative pose?' I asked. 'Is it just a symbol?'

'Of course it is a symbol,' said Daaji. 'Nevertheless, we also observe that even those who no longer require meditation still tend to maintain their meditation practice. Every morning, they still sit for meditation. Now, why would they do this? Is it because they enjoy it? Is it a habit? A formality?'

Daaji paused. 'You can think over this.'

The Meditative State

'Your meditation should never end,' said Daaji.

His words punctuated a long silence. 'Of course, this does not mean that you never get up again!' he continued. 'You cannot remain seated in meditation all day, but you can remain in a *meditative state* throughout all of your activities.

Your life becomes a meditation, you see—a dynamic and ongoing one. It is meditation with open eyes. You are not seated in meditation. Yet, you are meditating.

'In India, we have a concept called *Brahman.* Traditionally, Brahman is akin to God. It is thought to be the Ultimate Reality, the Supreme Being, or whatever you may like to call it. Yet, if we examine the etymological roots of the word, we uncover a different story. "Brahman" is derived from two Sanskrit roots: bruha and man. Bruha means "expansion", and man means "thinking" or "contemplation". So Brahman literally means "that which expands and contemplates".

'Let's step back for a moment. Do you remember how I described consciousness as a big circle?'

'Yes,' I said.

'The centre of the circle represents the deepest core of our being, and the circumference stands for our external awareness,' said Daaji. 'A time comes when consciousness expands in both directions simultaneously—toward the centre and the circumference. That is Brahman in the true sense. It is expansion, but it is also thinking, because the mind—which thinks—exists within consciousness.'

'So most people think Brahman to be something other than what it really is,' I said.

'Yes,' said Daaji. 'We have applied our human understanding to something that is beyond understanding. You see, one of the reasons that Socrates was executed was that he proclaimed the gods to be human creations. He observed that the gods, as they were presented, had human characteristics. Therefore, he concluded that they were human projections.

'While that was going on in Greece, the same thing was happening in India. It still is, in fact. And not just in India. It is a peculiar facet of human nature that we assign human qualities to everything, including God. You see, the Sanskrit word for individual being is *atman*. Atman literally means "that which moves and thinks". So you can see that the definition of an individual is very close to the ancients' definition of God. The only distinction is that one expands, while the other merely moves.

'Why are they so similar? The reason is that people thought, "God must be like us, but greater." If the individual being is something that moves, then God—being greater—must expand, for expansion is greater than mere movement. So they took the Ultimate and named it "Brahman", according to their human understanding.

'In reality, Brahman is not the Ultimate. It is the state in which consciousness contemplates and expands. The Ultimate is far beyond this. The Ultimate is changeless, so it cannot expand, contract, or contemplate.'

'So in the meditative state, our consciousness exhibits the qualities of Brahman,' I said, 'but that is not the Ultimate State.'

'Correct,' said Daaji. 'We have to go beyond Brahman. And there is a term for that too: *Parabrahman,* which means "beyond Brahman". And the state of Parabrahman is also just another stage in our journey. It is not the end. The meditative state keeps on evolving, you see. It grows finer and subtler until it dissolves into the Ultimate State. But it cannot evolve unless we create it in the first place.'

Daaji paused in reflection.

'I don't think anybody will be truly satisfied with meditation until the effect becomes permanent,' he said. 'Of what use is profound meditation if it doesn't transform your daily experience? Otherwise, meditation is like drawing water from a well using a leaky bucket. You're unable to retain it and carry it into your life.'

'How do we make the effects of meditation carry over?' I asked.

'The first step is to meditate,' he said. 'Meditation is the mother of the meditative state. Without a mother, there is no baby, and without the act of meditation, there is no meditative state. We achieve permanency in meditation through repeated meditations. With daily meditation, you steadily build that meditative condition. Brick by brick, meditation by meditation, you build it. If you don't meditate frequently, that condition starts to wane.'

'And then you have to create it all over again,' I said.

'Yes,' said Daaji. 'It's like a plant that requires daily water and sunshine. If you neglect it, you'll have to keep resuscitating it. How will it flourish?

'But it is not enough to meditate. You must also bring that meditative consciousness into your wakeful awareness. This depends on the way in which we conduct ourselves in the minutes that immediately follow meditation. A fresh meditative state is like wet cement. It needs some time to settle before you can carry it into your day. If you just jump out of your chair the very instant meditation ends, that meditative state of consciousness becomes fractured. This is akin to throwing it away. It's like working hard for a paycheck and then tossing it in the garbage! If you're going to do that, then why meditate at all?'

'So what do you recommend?' I asked.

'After meditation, open your eyes very gently,' he said. '*Then, remain in meditation for a few minutes more, but with half-open eyes.* This is very important. In those few minutes, you are not thinking about what you have to do today. You do not check the messages on your phone. You are still meditating—but with slightly open eyes. Stay like this for a few minutes, until you feel totally present in your surroundings.

'Even then, move slowly at first. Remain still. Remain meditative. Anything jarring should be completely avoided. You have to be like a deep-sea diver, slowly ascending from the watery depths. Nothing can be rushed! We should even refrain from drinking water immediately after meditation.'

'Why?' I asked.

'Whenever a person is upset, a drink of water helps to calm them down,' said Daaji. 'This shows us that water can change our inner condition. Now that may be good when someone is upset, but after meditation, we want to preserve the condition that we have. We don't want to change it. So we avoid drinking water for a few minutes. Along these same lines, if we have meditated with a fan blowing on us, we should keep that fan on for some time. We shouldn't immediately switch it off. And if it was off during meditation, it should stay off. Until that meditative condition is secure, we should do nothing that could possibly disturb it. Those first few minutes are critical. They determine the quality of your entire day.'

'What happens in these few minutes that makes them so important?' I asked.

'Your meditative consciousness merges into your normal waking state,' said Daaji. 'By spending just a few minutes meditating with open eyes, your consciousness remains meditative as you adjust to the waking state. After a short while, the two states coexist. You are inwardly absorbed, and you are perfectly alert to your surroundings. This is one aspect in converting the act of meditation into a state of meditativeness.

'When we meditate, we acquire new inner conditions. Acquiring a condition is like signing a lease on a house. You may live there, but that doesn't mean you own it. If you don't own it, can you stay there permanently? You see, we have to find a way to make these conditions ours. Otherwise, it's like trying to grasp a fistful of water. It just trickles through your fingers and disappears.'

'What is the best way to achieve ownership of a condition?' I asked.

'The first step is to be *aware* of our condition. We have to be aware that we have received something. The best time to develop this awareness is immediately after meditation. After meditation is over, simply observe yourself. Observe yourself minutely. How do you feel? Our condition can manifest in various ways. A journal can be an extremely useful tool because if you have to write about your condition, you will naturally be attentive to it. When you're attentive, your awareness becomes more finely tuned and your sensitivity increases. Initially, many people say that they don't know what to write. At first, you may only write one sentence, or even one word. But after a few weeks, you may write paragraphs. Soon, you'll fill pages with detailed descriptions.

'The more awareness we have of our condition, the more we will be able to experience its depth and intensity. A new condition is like a seed. It starts in a very small way and gradually unfolds. It expands from within and becomes *enlivened*.

Our entire being now seems to vibrate along with it. When the condition is sufficiently enlivened, it peaks. Then takes a new turn. We now start to absorb it, you see. We *imbibe* it. It starts to become a part of us. As it becomes part of us, our thoughts, feelings, and actions start to reflect its particular characteristics. One interesting facet of this process is that the more we imbibe the condition, the less intense it becomes. Its feeling starts to wane, you see. Eventually, we stop feeling it altogether. Then, we might think that we have lost it! But if you examine yourself carefully, you'll find that it is not gone. Instead of feeling it, you are *becoming* it.

'For example, look what happens when you eat a meal. Initially, you feel the presence of that food in your stomach. However, when the food is digested, you no longer feel it in your system. It is becoming a part of you. Similarly, the experience of any condition only proves that it has not yet become a part of you. It's still foreign. It's still a novelty. When it truly becomes a part of you, you are unable to experience it at all. As Babuji used to say, the eye cannot see itself.'

'It *is* itself,' I said.

'Exactly,' said Daaji. 'In that situation, the condition is truly secured. It has become yours.

You stay in this state of not feeling very much until your heart starts craving something new. That craving is what triggers the next condition.'

'And the entire cycle is repeated again,' I said.

'Yes,' said Daaji. 'This entire process of enlivening, imbibing, and securing the condition must become second nature. After all, there are so many conditions to traverse on this journey. As we move along, we also find that each condition is finer and subtler than the last. Unless our perception becomes continuously finer, these superfine conditions will elude us altogether. Then we won't be able to enliven them, what to say of imbibing or securing them by becoming one with them.'

'How can we make our perception more subtle?' I asked.

'It's like learning a new language,' said Daaji. 'Gradually, we pick it up, but only if we observe ourselves and pay keen attention to each condition as it comes. And I already described how we do that. But we have to start this habit at the earliest because at higher stages, the conditions are so subtle that they become almost impossible to perceive. If we cannot perceive them, they get stunted, and we cannot move forward. If, however, your inner senses have been progressively tuned over the course of your journey, you will be able to work with those superfine conditions. You will pass through them to still finer states, eventually arriving at the subtlest condition of all—the conditionless condition.'

'Often, we get distracted in the hustle and bustle of life,' I said. 'At those times, it can seem as if we lose the condition that we received in meditation. Can we get it back without meditating a second time?'

'You don't need to meditate a second time,' said Daaji. 'Just stop for a moment, close your eyes, and reconnect yourself to the heart. That automatically recalls your condition. Or, you can consciously recall what that condition felt like. By remembering it, we recreate it. In the morning, it might have taken you an entire hour to enter a state of deep meditation, but now, you can find yourself on the verge of samadhi in only a few seconds.'

'How is it that a condition that took an hour to develop can get recreated in just a few moments?' I asked.

'With your morning meditation, you have already forged the pathway,' said Daaji. 'Now that the path is established, you need only to follow it.

You just refer to your heart, and it comes. And the more you meditate, the easier this becomes.'

MEDITATION

- Sit comfortably, in a place where you can meditate without noise or distractions, preferably at the same time and place every day.
- Gently close your eyes. Centre your awareness in your heart, supposing that divine light is present there and that it is attracting you from within. Relax into that awareness. You may even relax into a deeper state, beyond awareness.
- Remain in meditation until you feel that it is complete. After meditation, slowly open your eyes. Remain in meditation for a few minutes more, but with slightly open eyes. Be still and observe how you feel. Note these observations in your journal. When you feel ready, you can stand up and go about your day.

4
Cleaning

THE CLEANING METHOD is a core practice of Heartfulness. Its purpose is to free us from patterns of thinking, emotional reactivity, and behavioural tendencies. The results of cleaning are tangible and immediate. In my experience, using the method for even a few minutes can have profound effects. I have found that it can instantly change my attitude, lift my mood, and broaden my perspective. Over the years, it has often helped me to disentangle myself from various thought patterns, strong emotions, and even compulsive behaviours.

One of the reasons that cleaning is so effective is that it addresses both the symptom and the cause. It not only frees us from the effects of mental and emotional complexity, but removes it by the root.

'How exactly does the cleaning method contribute to our transformation?' I asked Daaji.

'Let us understand the problem that we face,' he said. 'We observe that when water flows continuously over the same ground, it slowly carves out a channel for itself. Eventually, it can become a gushing river. Similarly, when we repeatedly think about something, our thought carves a channel in our mind. Whenever our thought moves there, it deepens that channel, easing the way for our thought to flow there again and again. In this way, a single thought can develop into a tendency of thinking.

'Our minds contain an untold number of such channels. They form a vast and complex network. When our thinking is confined to these beaten pathways, it becomes narrow and repetitive. We become more particular in our tastes and hardened in our opinions. As thought begets action, our mental tendencies further develop into behavioural habits.

'A tendency has its own momentum. It cannot be broken so easily. Often, we have trouble diverting the mind from its tendencies. Their pull is too strong! Instead, we usually fight with them. But that's like mud-wrestling an oiled pig—there's no way to win! If you want to change yourself, you cannot focus on the thing you want to change. That only strengthens the very tendency you want to do away with. Many parents know this. When training young children, we often give them negative commands. In many ways, we say, "should not, do not, avoid this, avoid that." Does it work? It usually makes them more obstinate. It's better to simply divert their attention. Rather than saying, "No chocolate", we say, "Let's have this instead." Instead of focusing on the negative, we focus on the positive. Instead of resolving not to tell lies, we simply tell the truth. But when the tendencies are strong, this approach also fails.

'You see, we must tackle our problems at the deepest level—the subconscious level. That is where the root of our problems lie. However, subconscious means "beneath consciousness". That means that the subconscious is largely inaccessible to conscious manipulation. We can change deliberate action—but subconscious action? It is subliminal. It occurs beneath the scope of our awareness. When we are barely even aware of something, how can we possibly change it? This is the biggest hurdle that we face when trying to work upon ourselves.'

'So dealing with subliminal thoughts requires a unique approach,' I said.

'Absolutely,' said Daaji. 'We do not generally realize the extent to which the subconscious affects our daily experience. We are unaware of its enormous influence and the way in which it drives our conscious awareness from moment to moment.

'But it is not a one-way relationship in which our conscious thoughts are mere products of subconscious influences. Rather, the relationship is cyclic.

'One way to understand the interaction between the subconscious mind and our conscious thoughts is by comparing it to a garden. A conscious thought is like a seed, sown into the fertile ground of the subconscious. That seed then germinates in the subconscious. Eventually, it blossoms into our conscious awareness and becomes an enduring pattern of similar thoughts. Just as a single seed produces a tree from which thousands of new seeds are grown, a single thought can grow into a tendency of thinking, through which we produce thousands of new thought-seeds. You can see how our consciousness can easily turn into a complex jungle!

'The cleaning method hits at the very root.

It is not about understanding or consciously re-programming our habits of thinking and behaviour. Instead, it works directly upon the subconscious. It is like weeding a garden. Whenever we pull up weeds, we must be sure to pull them out by their roots. If their roots remain in the ground, the weeds will continue to sprout, over and over again. Similarly, whatever we have already planted in the subconscious will continue to sprout in the form of thoughts and emotions. Unless we deal with those roots, our attempts at transformation often lead to frustration.'

Daaji paused.

'We have now referred to Patanjali's *Yoga Sutras* on a number of occasions. So far, we have spoken about each of the eight steps except for the first one: yama. Yama refers to the removal of unwanted tendencies. This is exactly what we achieve with the cleaning method. Through meditation, we create an inner environment where unwanted seeds cannot take root, but it is through the cleaning method that we fry up the existing seeds and pull out the complex root structures already embedded so deeply within.

'In yogic philosophy, thought-seeds that have already been planted in the subconscious are known as *samskaras*, or impressions.'

'Does every thought end up taking root in the subconscious and becoming an impression?' I asked.

'It is the thought's emotional content that gets planted—not the thought itself,' said Daaji. 'A samskara is your emotional memory. It is the emotion associated with that particular thought. We may not retain that memory at a conscious level—we may not retain the existential memory—but its *emotional* content certainly remains with us. Most of the time, that emotional content remains dormant. It's hidden away in the subconscious. However, when we encounter a situation that resonates with that particular emotion, that emotional state gets triggered. This produces similar thoughts to the parent thought—the thought with which the emotion was originally associated. When thoughts and emotions become repetitive, our reactions become habitual.'

'So our emotions create the samskaras that are planted in the subconscious,' I said.

'Yes,' said Daaji, 'but every thought has some emotional content. How much emotion it contains is only a matter of degree. Even if the emotion associated with a thought is not particularly intense, that thought will have at least a positive or negative flavour to it. No thought is completely neutral—to be completely neutral is to have no thoughts at all. That is a state of pure perception, of pure witnessing. The greater a thought's emotional intensity, the stronger its subconscious influence. That samskara, or impression, would be stronger.

'We often associate thought with the mind and emotion with the heart. However, I prefer to view it as a heart-mind field because there can be no emotion without thinking and no thinking without emotion. With spiritual practice, however, a time comes when the heart becomes completely unbiased, when it has no likes or dislikes, no preferences or prejudice. That is when the mind transcends thinking and becomes a mere witness, perceiving reality directly. Until then, our thoughts affect our heart, and the heart's activity produces thoughts in the mind.'

'What determines a thought's emotional content?' I asked.

'The ego,' said Daaji. 'The ego is our sense of self. It is the feeling of "I-ness". To truly understand its role in creating impressions, you'll have to permit me to digress for a moment and go into greater depth on this topic of ego.'

'Yes, please,' I said.

'Okay,' said Daaji. 'The ego's only motive is self-preservation. It fears being extinguished, you see. Therefore, it constantly works to bolster itself, to increase itself.

'The ego is a funny thing. When someone asks where we feel things, we point to the heart. If someone asks where we think things, we point to the head. Where is the ego? It doesn't really exist anywhere. Yet, it tends to dominate our lives.

'Since the ego doesn't exist in any tangible way, it secures its position through what it considers to be its possessions. For instance, you buy a big house, and your ego declares, "I am this." It has measured and quantified itself through that particular possession. This is how it proves its existence to itself.

'However, "possessions" doesn't only mean material belongings. Rather, it refers to anything that the ego has claimed as its own. The ego says, "my nationality, my language, my culture, my body, my intellect, my ideology". It doesn't matter whether something actually belongs to you or not. Does anything really belong to us? Even the soul is not ours! The ego appropriates. It identifies itself with something and feels a sense of ownership over it.

'Now, this feeling of "mine-ness" has a side effect. When we feel that something is ours, we develop expectations. "My business should be successful. My spouse should be attractive. My car should be luxury." You don't care about another person's business, spouse, or car. But when your ego is invested, you care very much. When our expectations are met or exceeded, we are happy, and we react positively. When they are unmet, we react negatively.'

'So without the ego's involvement, there are no emotional reactions, and hence, no impressions.'

'That's right,' said Daaji. 'The ego feels entitled to certain outcomes, based upon its sense of perceived ownership. Then it reacts accordingly, and we form impressions. Remember that a reaction is either positive or negative. It is either toward something or against something. Every reaction contains either like or dislike, attraction or aversion, desire or fear. There is no such thing as a neutral reaction because to be neutral is to not react.'

'So you're saying that emotion comes from the ego?' I asked.

'Yes, emotion comes from the ego, but not feeling,' said Daaji. 'Emotion has bias. It likes some things and dislikes others. Feeling, on the other hand, has no preferences or prejudice. It is generous and accepting because it comes from the heart. Subdue ego, and true feeling naturally emerges.

'These emotional reactions do not leave us unscathed. We always receive the brunt of our reactions. They affect our consciousness and manifest as emotional and psychological states.'

'And this happens because of points A, B, C, and D,' I said.

In the chest area, there are four points, which we call A, B, C, and D. These four points determine the exact effect that a reaction will have on us. Babuji discovered points A and B in 1945. Points C and D came to light more recently. Daaji says that even now, many facets of the subtle, spiritual anatomy are being revealed to us.

Daaji publicly revealed the locations of points C and D in 2015. He had already mentioned their existence to me in private, but not their locations. One day, I wrote to him to find out where they are. He replied:

'Please locate them yourself and send your findings to me.'

After spending a day internally researching their positions, I drew a diagram of where I thought them to be, which I sent to Daaji.

He wrote back, saying, 'Move them a bit toward the right, and it will be correct. But do not share this, or it will rob others of the joy of discovering something new!'

However, now that the positions of these points are public knowledge, they can be shared. To locate points A, B, C, and D, start at the base of the sternum, where the rib cage cavity begins. Measure one finger width down from the sternum (using

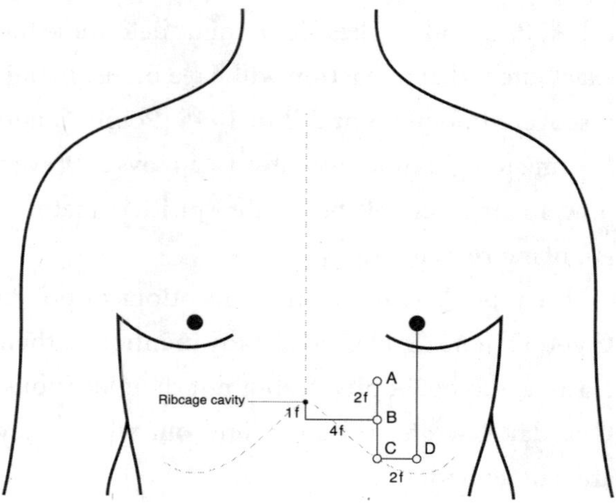

your own fingers). Then go four finger widths to the left. This is the location of point B. Two fingers above point B is point A. Point C is on the bottom rib, directly below point B. Point D is two fingers to the left of point C, directly underneath the left nipple.

'The functions of these four points are critical,' Daaji said. 'They are closely connected to the heart, and the heart is largely responsible for our mental and emotional state. Now, whenever we react to something with like or dislike, specific vibrations emerge at point C. You can actually feel them. I hope people will try to notice it. Now, depending on the intensity of our reaction—and the nature of its vibrations—a ripple effect is created. That ripple takes those vibrations from point C to either point A, B, or D.

'Point A is associated with material life, so whenever our reaction concerns a worldly like or dislike, the vibrations at point C ripple to point A. As a result, point A becomes disrupted.'

'What happens when point A is disrupted?' I asked.

'Suppose you see a beautiful apartment and say, "What a nice apartment,"' said Daaji. 'That feeling of liking makes a rather light impression.

As a result, the vibration at point C is also light, and its ripple effect to point A—the seat of material desires—is weak. But then, you brood over this thought and think, *I would like to stay in this apartment.* Now, the vibration at point C becomes a little stronger, and this is also reflected at point A. You brood over it even more and become insistent. *I have to have this apartment!* you think. Now that disturbance becomes very big, and your emotional state becomes extreme. You are now fixated on fulfilling that desire. You may also be worried about not satisfying it. In either case, you become restless and that restlessness robs you of your peace.

'Let's look at point B. This point is associated with sexuality. Whenever we react according to the sexual urge, the vibrations from point C ripple to point B. This rouses a feeling of passion.

'Point D is the guilt point. When we ignore our conscience, guilt forms at point D. The effect of guilt is extreme heaviness in the system. Guilt not only arises because of our wrong actions, but because of our *inactions.* For instance, suppose that you're a doctor and you see an injured person by the side of the road. Yet, you continue on your way. *Let someone else help them,* you think. The next day, you read in the newspaper that the person died.

Nobody stopped to help them! I think that this guilt would haunt you all your life. The guilt arising from inactions is somehow more poignant than the guilt resulting from wrong actions.

'The vibrations that are present in points A, B, C, and D gradually settle, or condense, producing what Babuji referred to as *grossness*. These points can only handle so much grossness. They become saturated, you see. When these points cannot handle any more grossness, the grossness evaporates and lands at yet other points, which we need not discuss right now because it's another subject altogether. However, the result is that we experience a cascade of psychological and emotional effects.'

'And the cleaning method clears these disturbances,' I said.

'Yes,' said Daaji. 'As a result, our psychological profile normalizes, our emotions become balanced, and our mind ceases to fixate on that particular emotion.'

'What happens when we don't have a method to clean ourselves?' I asked.

'Have you ever seen what happens to a field when it is left untended?' he asked.

'It becomes overgrown,' I said.

'And it eventually turns back into forest,' said Daaji. 'When samskaras are not removed, they develop unabated. They continue to strengthen and even give birth to new samskaras.'

'How does this process occur?' I asked.

'Suppose that you are walking down the street one day and a stranger insults you. Does that insult affect you or not? It depends on you. One person laughs it off, but another person wants to fight. Somebody else might brood over it all day long. So we see that while certain people may react to a particular stimulus, others will not. Amongst those who do react, their reactions can be different—even when the stimulus is the same. If each person can have a unique reaction to the same stimulus—or no reaction at all—can you pin the entire blame on that stimulus?'

'No,' I said.

'It is a combination of the stimulus and something *inside you* that prompts your reaction,' said Daaji. 'Unless you are already predisposed to be affected by that type of stimulus, it cannot have any effect on you. That something inside you is your samskara.

'You see, for all mental and emotional states, there are primal and proximal causes. The primal cause is the inner influence, the subconscious influence that is already inside you—your samskara. In this case, it represents a predisposition to react to the insult in a particular way. Suppose that the insult irritates you. The primal cause is the samskara, or impression, that causes you to become irritated. The proximal cause is the outer influence—the stimulus. It is the spark that ignites the gasoline.'

'The insult,' I said.

'Yes,' said Daaji. 'And it can be any stimulus. But no matter what that trigger may be, you will not react without one. Your samskara—the primal, inner cause—does not get triggered without an external stimulus, the proximal cause. Without a proximal cause, your irritation remains dormant. It is like a snake in the grass, lying silently and waiting for just the right moment, for just the right environment. Then, when a proximal cause comes along, that samskara roars to life. It rises up and becomes the catalyst for your reaction.

'You asked how samskaras develop. The answer is that new samskaras are built on the backs of old ones. Suppose, God forbid, that a snake bites someone. As a result, he develops a phobia of snakes. But really, that fear is not a fear of snakes.

It is the fear of death *in the guise of a snake*. The snakebite is a proximal cause. It triggers his pre-existing samskara to fear death. On top of that samskara, he now has a new one: the fear of snakes.

'The formation of samskaras is progressive, you see. New ones are offshoots of previous ones. It is like the process by which we learn. If you don't know the alphabet, you can't possibly read Shakespeare. If you don't know some physics, you can't understand Richard Feynman. Similarly, what we make of the world around us depends upon our previous experiences.'

'But not every impression comes as a result of our experiences,' I said. 'For instance, in your example, a snakebite caused a person to develop a phobia of snakes. But phobias don't always arise out of personal experience. A person can be afraid of snakes without ever having been bitten.'

'Some try to make sense of these things in a fantastical way,' said Daaji. 'They'll say that such a person must have been bitten by a snake in a previous life! But that is a lazy argument. For instance, so many people are afraid of flying. By the same logic, they must have been in plane crashes in previous lives. But airplanes have only existed for the last one hundred years! So that can't be the answer. Phobias do arise from our experiences, but an experience need not materialize for it to feel real to us. For example, you can imagine a frightening snake and start to feel afraid. The snake isn't real, but the emotion is. Your imagination triggers a very real fear of death. When that thought gets connected to your underlying fear, it automatically becomes a phobia. This isn't only true of fear and phobias. When any thought becomes connected to an existing samskara, a new samskara can be formed.

'Samskaras are like trees. Let's take the fear of death again. That is the tree's trunk. From that trunk, new branches sprout. Those are your phobias. That tree is the sum-total of all your impressions related to fear. It is a network of fear, a dynamic of fear in your consciousness.'

'And our consciousness is filled with many other kinds of trees!' I remarked.

'Yes,' said Daaji, 'and from each tree, a new tree can grow. Ultimately, our consciousness can become a complex jungle! Each samskara takes up real estate in consciousness. Our energies get completely tied up in these samskaric patterns. They dominate our thinking and guide our pursuits. As our samskaric jungle grows denser, our consciousness deadens. Its energies are tied up, its space filled.

'Earlier, we spoke about how the human system gets saturated with grossness.'

'Hardened impressions,' I said.

'Yes,' said Daaji. 'Well, nature now intervenes and purges this grossness from our system through a process known as *bhoga*. Bhoga means "experience". In life, we undergo so many kinds of experiences. Yogic philosophy tells us that these experiences are only bhoga. They are effects of our past impressions, which we now must undergo in a tangible way.'

'However, we generally react to this process of undergoing bhoga (or in other words, our life experiences). As a result of these reactions, we form fresh samskaras.'

'So the process is never-ending,' I said. 'We create impressions, they come to fruition as life experiences, and then we form new impressions from those experiences. It seems as if bhoga only perpetuates impressions, instead of freeing us from them.'

'*We* perpetuate them,' said Daaji. 'When we feel as if we are suffering for no reason, we react. You see, we generally become confused and embittered when undergoing miseries. “Why?” we ask. We complain to God, saying, “What the hell are you doing?” These reactions not only create new impressions, but also make us toxic from inside and deflect the grace that descends from above. Also, bhoga doesn’t only come in the form of suffering. Enjoyment is also a manifestation of bhoga. But remember: any reaction creates an impression!’

‘So bhoga is only helpful if we don’t react to it,’ I said.

‘Yes,’ said Daaji. ‘Then it is immensely helpful. That is the wisdom of remaining serene and cheerful under all circumstances.’

He stood up, removed one of Babuji’s books from his shelf, and began to read:

> The external help comes in the form of suffering caused by the wrongs done by others, against which the people generally poison their thought on account of their own ignorance. This is very improper because this action, having helped the process of purification, has in fact put you under a sense of obligation. When this is the case, the work done through an external agency, it may be any, has in other words rendered the function of a true friend (Chandra: 2009).

'However,' said Daaji, 'we can't condemn ourselves or others as having invited our fates, whatever they may be. We can't point the finger and say, "You brought this on yourself by creating samskaras." I have actually witnessed examples of this, where people withhold help from a suffering person while saying, "I cannot interfere with nature." This is inhuman. It is our duty to interfere with peoples' suffering, in order to relieve it. Even worse would be to mistreat someone while crookedly professing that you are helping to purify them! Then, there are also traditions in which people self-castigate. This is a negative approach, which will certainly create more complexity in us. We don't need to invite suffering. Yet, when suffering is unavoidable, we must be able to accept it warmly with a cheerful attitude.'

'Is this like the idea of karma, in which we are supposed to undergo the consequences of our past actions?' I asked.

'We actually undergo the consequences of our samskaras—not of our actions,' said Daaji. 'If you act without creating any impression at all, there will be no consequence. You will not partake of its effect in any way. It is only the samskara that causes this famous boomerang effect. For example, suppose that you purchase something, and later, you decide to return it. Without the bill of sale, you have no basis to collect a refund. An impression is like a cosmic bill of sale. It links our action to its result. Without the impression, that action can never return to us. Remember that bhoga is nature's way of removing impressions. If there is no impression to remove, there is no bhoga to undergo.

'We should understand that the purpose of bhoga is not to punish or reward us. Nor does bhoga exist to teach us lessons. There is a famous story from the Mahabharata. The great warrior Bhishma was felled in battle. As he lay mortally wounded upon a bed of arrows, Lord Krishna approached him. "What has led me to such a death?" Bhishma asked. "I have examined a hundred of my previous lives, and I see nothing that could be the cause of this fate."

"Look beyond it," said Krishna.

"I cannot see beyond it," said Bhishma.

"But I can," said Krishna. "In one life, you were a prince. One day, you took a snake by its tail, spun it around, and threw it. It then fell on a thorny bush, where it died. It is the effect of that deed that you are facing now. That is why these arrows have become your deathbed."

'Now, if the consequence of Bhishma's action had come immediately, he would have understood the correlation between his action and its result. In that case, he could have learned something from it and corrected himself. But when so much time elapses between a cause and its effect, we are not aware of their relationship. We miss the causality at work. When this is the case, how can we learn anything from the experience?

'So nature is not trying to teach us lessons. It only frees us from the weight of our impressions so that our consciousness may remain pure and light.'

'Why does nature want to remove our samskaras?' I asked.

'Nature's regulatory purpose is to keep its systems pure,' said Daaji. 'When impressions settle in the subconscious, they form a vibratory buffer between consciousness and soul. Impressions do not touch the soul, but they form a layer around it. This causes us to remain isolated from the inner Source. This situation represents an imperfection in nature.

'But nature's process of bhoga grinds along slowly. Through bhoga, impressions are removed individually, and we have to undergo the effects of each one. This takes time, and we suffer a lot in the process. Meanwhile, we add new impressions at a faster rate than the old ones can be removed!

'Our impressions are also too numerous to be exhausted over the course of a single lifetime through bhoga alone. That is why so many Eastern spiritual traditions insist that one lifetime is not enough to free us from their effects. But when we remove impressions in bulk through cleaning, the entire load can be wiped out with a portion of this very life.'

'In the yogic literature that I've read, I've never come across any method for removing samskaras,' I said. 'Instead, the focus seems to be on replacing negative samskaras with positive ones.'

'Samskara is impurity,' said Daaji. 'Can there be good impurity and bad impurity? There is only impurity. A good person's samskaras compel them to perform good deeds. A bad person's samskaras compel them to perform bad deeds. Are these two people so different from one another? Both are in chains. The only difference is that one chain is golden, while the other is wrought of iron. Whether a chain is made of iron or gold, it binds us just the same. That is why we do not differentiate between good and bad samskaras. The Heartfulness cleaning method also does not discriminate. Whether good or bad, everything goes.'

'Does this mean that we have no free will?' I asked. 'Are we simply at the mercy of our samskaras?'

'Not at all,' said Daaji. 'We certainly have free will, and in fact, that is our problem! You see, we always retain the freedom to follow our hearts' pure signals or to ignore them and surrender to the pull of our samskaras instead. That is our choice, and so the responsibility is also ours.'

'So there are two aspects to handling samskaras,' I said. 'One is to remain connected to the heart and not react to the samskaric pull. The other aspect is to remove samskaras through the cleaning process or by undergoing bhoga.'

'Yes,' said Daaji. 'And through cleaning, we remove the impressions in bulk, as opposed to bhoga, in which they are removed individually. Furthermore, cleaning removes impressions before they can manifest as experiences. To remove them without having to undergo them is like having an operation under anesthesia. We don't experience it at all.

'An even deeper cleaning occurs when we meditate along with a Heartfulness trainer. In fact, the foundation of our samskaric edifice is completely removed in our very first sitting with a trainer. No edifice can stand without an intact foundation. It is bound to collapse, sooner or later.

'In this process of purification, our role is to perform our own individual cleaning at the end of each day. By doing so, we remove that particular day's worth of samskaric accumulation. By continuing to take regular sittings with a trainer, we can exhaust our samskaric load within a portion of our life.

'Yet, despite the fact that we clean our samskaras day by day and take sittings a few times per month, the load won't get any lighter unless we also stop creating new impressions. Otherwise, it's like bailing out a leaky boat without bothering to repair the hole.'

'And that means being non-reactive,' I said.

'Yes,' said Daaji.

'How can we become non-reactive?' I asked.

'Meditate,' said Daaji. 'In meditation, we learn to ignore our thoughts. We do not entertain them, nor do we fight with them. They are like mere dreams passing before us. When we become as non-reactive in the waking state as we are during meditation, we cease forming impressions altogether. Then real freedom dawns. We do not have to try to remain meditative because there is nothing inside us to react to so many external stimuli. We move from instinct to intuition, from the subconscious to the superconscious, from the reactive mind to the responsive heart.'

Doing the Cleaning

The cleaning method is a valuable tool with many practical applications. It helps us go beyond our personal limits and prevents us from getting tripped up in life's overwhelming complexity. There are so many occasions when the cleaning has saved me from making big mistakes in life. Just a few minutes of cleaning allows for so much clarity and wisdom to dawn.

'I think that the cleaning method is possibly the most important of all the Heartfulness practices,' said Daaji. 'Chariji used to say that meditating without cleaning is like having a fancy car that's stuck in the mud. A supercar won't do you much good without a decent road! Similarly, no matter how much you meditate, you won't get very far without cleaning, because the beautiful inner state that you create will remain covered by so many layers of impurity.

'Nevertheless, we should never think ourselves to be impure or unclean. With the cleaning method, we move toward purity without ever thinking ourselves to be impure. We move toward simplicity without ever thinking ourselves to be complex. Beneath our samskaras, we are already pure and simple! Impurity never touches the soul, you see. It only obscures it and prevents its divine rays from illuminating our consciousness. When that is the case, our awareness diminishes. We become less cognizant. We only have to remove impurity and complexity, and our natural state of purity and simplicity begins to emerge.'

'So we should just do the cleaning as a matter of routine,' I said.

'Correct,' said Daaji. 'Do it in the same spirit that you take a bath or shower—as a habit of good hygiene. To bathe or brush your teeth is a matter of outer hygiene. The cleaning is all about inner hygiene. It makes your consciousness crystal clear.'

'When you say impurities, you mean samskaras, right?' I asked.

'Yes,' said Daaji. 'But this is all within the realm of theory and philosophy. When you actually do the cleaning, you feel so light afterward. You feel so fresh. It is a tangible feeling. That feeling motivates you, regardless of whether you are convinced by the theory of samskaras or not. I think that the feeling of lightness is the reason that most people use this method. They feel a difference in themselves, which they appreciate.

'Over time, we also find changes in ourselves. Many habits and tendencies simply drop off. Sometimes, you don't even notice that they are gone. Then somebody says, "What happened to you, man? You used to be so irritated all the time." "Oh, really?" you say. You don't even remember it.

'Normally, we perform the cleaning for fifteen to thirty minutes in the evening. However, there are times when we shouldn't wait till the end of the day. Perhaps you get in an argument, or you see something that leaves you shaken. In such cases, sit down and clean immediately—even if just for two to three minutes. See, if you spilled ketchup all over your shirt at lunchtime, would you wait till the evening to clean it or to change your clothes? You wouldn't. It's the very same thing. Don't carry around that stain on your consciousness all day. Don't carry that heavy burden unnecessarily. Take care of it immediately. If something extreme happens and you feel very disturbed, contact a Heartfulness trainer and request a sitting. They'll meditate along with you, aiding you with yogic transmission.

'When we take a sitting with a trainer, they perform cleaning on us as we meditate. The cleaning we receive from a trainer is a deeper cleaning than what we achieve during our daily individual practice. When receiving a sitting, we simply meditate and let the trainer do their own work. We do not use the cleaning method at that time because the trainer is already doing it on our behalf. But when we use the cleaning method on our own, we avoid meditating at that time. We just do the cleaning, as per the method.'

'How can we be sure that we are cleaning, rather than meditating?' I asked.

'In meditation, you can just let yourself relax deeper and deeper into it,' said Daaji. 'But cleaning is a more active process. In cleaning, we use the will to throw everything out, so when we sit for cleaning, we must remain alert.

'But the best thing is to avoid creating impressions in the first place!' Daaji said with a laugh. 'Certain situations are bound to create samskaras—an argument, for example. Before the argument starts, you already know what's going to happen. You know that you won't like what the other person says. That's when you need awareness. Before the difficult conversation even begins, inoculate yourself with compassion and understanding toward the other person. But you also have to understand yourself! You know how you are likely to react, so put a check on yourself at that time.

'Normally, we think that cleaning is curative in nature. You use it to clean yourself and normalize your inner state. But cleaning can also be preventative. Once, in the eighties, I was working in my first pharmacy in New York. At that time, there was an intern working with us who was a newly married man. He had recently started meditation, too. One of his duties was to deliver medicines to nursing homes and hospitals, where he would meet the nurses who would then distribute the medications to the patients. One day, he came back with a red face. "Kamlesh, I am in big trouble," he said. "What happened?" I asked. "This nurse is after me. She is gorgeous! She is so beautiful! My heart is pumping, but I'm married. I should not even be thinking about it, but I want to meet her. See, she has given me the key to her apartment. I am supposed to see her tonight."

'I said, "I am sorry, I cannot help you." Too many things were going on at that time, you see. But then I had an idea. "Let's write a letter to

Chariji." He said, "By the time I write the letter and it comes back, it will be too late—she is expecting me tonight!" At that time, the fax machine was a new thing, so I told him, "Okay, write the letter, and we'll fax it to him." It was daytime in New York, so in India, where Chariji was at that time, it was the middle of the night. However, he would sleep with the fax machine right next to the bed. So, this intern wrote a letter. "Please help me. I am not able to resist this." Almost instantly, the reply came back: "Sit down and do the cleaning for five minutes. Then refer to your heart." So I said, "Go to the office and do it there." So he went, finished his cleaning, came back, and said, "Kamlesh, I shouldn't have written that letter." I asked him why not. He said, "Now the desire is gone, and I will have to miss the opportunity!"

'You see, when we clean, desires get weakened and clarity dawns. If he had met that young lady, he would likely have formed strong impressions and ended up feeling guilty. So cleaning is also preventative.

'Now suppose you've had a stressful day at work. By the time you arrive home, you're already in a reactive state. Maybe your wife has also had a tough day, so she's also reactive. What do you think is going to happen when you interact? Fireworks! So the best thing to do is to clean that baggage away, first thing. Do it as soon as you reach home, and your interactions will be more peaceful, more loving.

'You know those children's toys ... tops? When a top spins on its axis, it's not easy to knock it over. You can only knock it down when it's already unbalanced, when it's already wobbling on its axis. Most often, this is our condition when we come home in the evening. We're already wobbling on our axis. So before we have a chance to react, we stabilize ourselves by doing the cleaning. Otherwise, it's like returning home sweaty from the gym and immediately hugging your family! No matter how much they love you, they'd definitely prefer you to take a shower first! After you do your cleaning, you're fit to interact with others, both for your sake and for theirs. You see, we have to be careful with others. My actions and attitudes should not create impressions in other people. This is especially true if they don't have a method by which to remove samskaras. We have a method of cleaning ourselves. If we create a samskara, we can remove it. That isn't true for others. If they form an impression, they don't have an easy way of removing it.

'We can even help others simply by doing our own cleaning. Many of our samskaras are collective samskaras. For instance, family members often display common tendencies and traits. These are the result of shared samskaras. Now, by cleaning that particular samskara from yourself, you weaken it in the others, too. Removing your own part of a collective samskara is like removing the bottom layer of a mountain. Eventually, the entire formation will crumble and collapse.'

'So when we clean ourselves, we are also cleaning others,' I said.

'Yes,' said Daaji, 'but indirectly. Now, just imagine if millions of people did cleaning. You would start to witness very rapid change in the world!'

CLEANING

- Sit in a comfortable pose with the intention to remove all the impressions you have accumulated during the day.
- Close your eyes. Imagine that all the complexities and impurities are leaving your entire system.

- They are flowing out behind you, from the area between your tailbone and the top of your head.
- Feel that they are leaving you in the form of smoke or vapour.
- Remain alert. Gently accelerate the process with confidence and determination, applying your will as needed. If your attention drifts and other thoughts come to mind, gently bring your focus back to the cleaning.

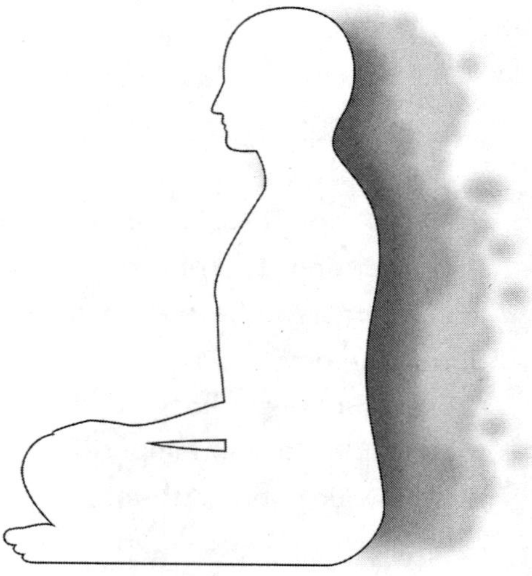

- Continue this process for approximately twenty to thirty minutes. You will know that it is finished when you start to feel a subtle lightness in your heart.
- Now suppose that a current of purity is coming from the Source and entering your system from the front. This current is flowing throughout your system, carrying away any remaining complexities and impurities.

- Let this continue for a minute or two.
- You have now returned to a simpler, purer, and more balanced state. Every cell of your body is emanating simplicity, lightness, and purity. Finish with the conviction that the cleaning has been completed effectively.

5

Prayer

THE THIRD MAIN practice of Heartfulness is a specific prayer that we offer twice per day. However, we can also offer our own prayers at any time, according to our heart's inspirations.

Prayer is spirituality's beating heart. Amidst so many spiritual ways, prayer represents a commonality. Although its practice and purpose may take different forms, prayer remains an essential way to connect with something higher than ourselves. If we approach prayer with just the right attitude, it transcends itself and becomes a way of *being*—a permanent, prayerful state that pervades all our activities.

While walking with Daaji in the woods, I asked him a question: 'What is prayer?'

'It is the inner cry of the heart,' said Daaji. 'The heart's feeling cannot be manipulated by the logical mind. Generally, we pray when we lack something. To pray under dire circumstances when we can bear no more is natural. But when we are happy and overjoyed, that feeling also becomes a prayer if we connect ourselves with God at that moment and express gratitude. In this situation, you are not asking. You are only sharing your joy, just as you would share your sorrow with an inner cry.'

'But in many cases, prayer *is* asking,' I said.

'This is due to our fears and desires,' said Daaji. 'Because of our fears, we seek divine protection and because of our desires, we seek a divine provider. This gives rise to a conception of a God who fulfills both of these functions. Viewing God as our protector and provider, we pray accordingly. "Oh Lord, please protect me from illness," or "Dear God, please bless me with a job." Thus, each person views God according to the particular kind of help that they need. For example, a weak person sees God as the giver of strength, and a sick person sees God as the giver of health. But God is none of these. These conceptions are merely projections of our own needs. This is one of the reasons that Lord Buddha never spoke about God. His idea was that if you could cut fear and desire, all our fantasies about God would disappear in one stroke. He was correct in his view. Until that happens, our ideas of God are mere fancies.'

'Then what is God?' I asked.

Daaji laughed and said, 'Someone once came to Babuji with a question. "Can you show me God?" What was Babuji's reply? "Supposing that I showed Him to you, how would you know that it was God?"

'It's like a small child who asks their mother, "Where did I come from?" The mother only says, "You will know one day." Such things are revealed at an opportune moment, when we are ready.'

'If to perceive God we must move beyond the shackles of imagination, then isn't using the masculine gender to refer to God a form of limitation as well?' I asked.

'It's a term with which everyone is familiar,' said Daaji. 'It is not a description of God. God is beyond description. Neither masculine nor feminine, God has no name, form, or attribute. Really, it's impossible to speak about God without telling a lie.'

After we had walked a little further, he said, 'I'll tell you a story that Babuji often narrated.'

Daaji proceeded to tell the tale of an ascetic monk who went to seek alms from a king. Arriving at the king's palace, the ascetic was informed that the king was occupied in prayer. However, since the ascetic was a holy man, he would be allowed to sit with the king as he prayed. The ascetic was led to the prayer room. Noticing the arrival of a holy man, the king turned to the ascetic and welcomed him but asked for his patience, as he had not yet completed his prayers. The ascetic sat with him, quietly observing.

'Oh Lord,' prayed the king, 'please grant me victory over my enemies. Grant me more territories, make my kingdom wealthy, and make me a great king.' The king continued in this manner for a few minutes, when all of a sudden, the ascetic stood up and started making his way to the door.

'Wait!' said the king. 'You have only just arrived. Why do you now take leave?'

'Your Highness,' said the ascetic to the king, 'I had come to beg alms from you, but now I see that you are a beggar, just as I am. So I will go and beg from the one from whom you are begging!'

'To grovel on our knees seeking blessings and benefits is a somewhat crass affair,' said Daaji. 'We can equate praying for personal enrichment to a situation in which a person marries for money. The relationship is cheapened. It matters little whether the benefits we seek are material or spiritual in nature. In both cases, such an approach would be against the heart's etiquette.

'For example, some people approach the Ultimate for fear of being condemned to hell. Others approach Him out of temptation for the heavenly abode. But to seek any return on love is sacrilege. In so doing, we damage our relationship with our Maker. At best, it becomes like a business relationship, and at worst, it is bribery. This is why the notion of "love for love's sake" has been so highly extolled. A true lover of the Lord has no ulterior motives. They care nothing for heaven or hell, for blessings or spiritual advancement. They are content with love. Do not ask for mere gifts when you can have the Giver. Only love can make this possible.

'Suppose, for instance, that you give a gift to someone you love. You think and think about what would suit them best. You buy it and lovingly wrap it. However, when presenting it to your loved one, that person snatches it out of your hands, rips off the paper, and rushes away with it—all without any acknowledgment. How do you think that would make you feel? They accepted your gift while ignoring its giver. Well, if you really love that person, you won't mind at all. However, they have missed the point of your gift.

'To give is an act of love, and as such, its purpose is to bring the giver and receiver together. A blessing has no meaning if it doesn't lead to a state of intimacy with the Giver. As another example, take the case of a person who endears himself to a rich relative in order to become their heir. He may get the inheritance, but he also loses a lot in the process! The sanctity of the relationship is ruined.

'If you truly seek the Giver, then forget about gifts. Forget about blessings. Forget about spiritual attainment. They will come in their own way; they should not preoccupy us. Anyway, when He is in your heart, for what could you possibly want? That is why some people pray only for *Him*.'

'What makes Him respond to such a noble prayer?' I asked. 'What makes Him offer Himself to us?' I asked.

'He is always offering Himself!' said Daaji. 'It is His nature to do so. At the same time, we observe that even though His blessings, His transmission, and His grace are always available, there is a big difference between a drizzle and a torrential downpour.'

'Then what is it that allows Him to pour Himself into us, rather than to bless us in drops and trickles?' I asked.

'Babuji quoted one poem,' said Daaji. 'O, thou thirsty for the divine intoxication! Empty thy heart for the purpose, for the head of the bottle of wine bows down only over an empty cup' (Chandra: 2009).

'So we must be empty in order to be filled,' I said.

'Yes,' said Daaji. 'When our hearts are already full, what space is there for anything else? Rather, we must create a vacuum in our hearts. A vacuum attracts. You know how rain is created?'

'It comes when there's low atmospheric pressure,' I said.

'Yes,' said Daaji. 'It creates a vacuum, and when there is a vacuum, the surrounding air gets sucked in, and it rises. Condensation forms, and then the rains fall. So if you seek a divine downpour, you must create a low-pressure system in your own heart. This means that your heart must be empty, divested of all desires for gifts, blessings, and attributes. Then, an inner vacuum is created. This automatically attracts the divine downpour that you seek. And when the vacuum in your heart is total, the Ultimate takes up residence there. He cannot avoid it.'

'But a vacuum need not attract only good things!' I said.

Daaji laughed. 'True,' he said. 'If the heart has even one little desire, a vacuum can attract trouble. The heart may be infinite, but the presence of a single desire can infinitely fill its space. In that case, the heart seeks its fulfillment in the mundane. Immediately, the world rushes in, and the vacuum is spoiled. A little carelessness and one is sure to pay the price! To have a vacuum in the heart is good, but only if the heart is oriented toward the Higher.'

'So when you say "inner vacuum", you mean a desireless state,' I said.

'It's more than that,' said Daaji. 'It's a total lack of oneself. You see, Plato said, "Know thyself", but Babuji had a different idea. He said, "Forget thyself!"

'After all, Lord Christ said that it is the simple and meek who reach heaven. Normally, we take this to mean that they reach heaven after death, but the fact is that into such hearts that are simple, innocent, and egoless, heaven descends automatically. Wherever such individuals go, they create heavens around them.

'But when the heart is already perfectly content, what further contentment could heaven bring? In yogic terminology, this state of perfect contentment is called *uparati*. In uparati, we desire nothing in this world, nor do we wish for anything in the next. You see, we usually understand contentment as the satisfaction of a desire. For instance, if you eat a five-course meal, could you want anything more? You are filled up! However, that is not uparati because tomorrow you will be hungry again. Rather, true contentment is to have no desires to fulfill. You become free from them. Previously, you were their slave. You worked continuously for their fulfillment. Now you are free. So this also tells us what the opposite of contentment is!'

'Yes,' I said, 'to be tormented by desires!'

'And it is according to these desires that most of us pray,' said Daaji, 'like the king from Babuji's story. And the desires that we aim to fulfill tend to be of four specific varieties. In the yogic tradition, these four aims are known as *artha, kama, dharma,* and *moksha*. These aims are also associated with points A, B, C, and D, which we spoke about previously, in the context of cleaning impressions.

'First, let's speak about artha, which is the desire for material fulfillment. This is a natural urge, covering our most basic needs: food, clothing, and shelter. But it can also manifest as a tendency to accumulate more and more. We buy clothes, houses, cars, electronics—you name it. Now, whether we are preoccupied with the latest smartphone or we are worried about paying the bills, it creates samskaric vibrations that ripple to point A.

'But with meditation, our external, material focus gets diverted inward—not completely, but to the necessary extent. As a result, we no longer feel the need to seek contentment outside ourselves. We have found it within! Now, we cannot worry so much about our problems either. Our perspective widens, you see.'

'And so our prayers no longer reflect that outward tendency,' I said.

'Right,' said Daaji. 'Meditation transforms us totally. This transformation manifests in many ways.

'The next kind of desire is for sexual satisfaction, which is known as kama. The desire for kama forms impressions that settle at point B, creating passion.'

'In just about every religion, there seems to be a tradition of celibacy,' I said. 'Should we avoid satisfying kama-based desires? Do you advocate that people reserve sex for procreation, for instance?'

'I'll share one incident with you,' said Daaji. 'Once, when I was travelling in north India, an old man came to see me with a burning question. "Why is it that every time I have ever had sex, I felt guilty afterward?" he asked. "Precisely because you only satisfy yourself and have never once thought about the other," I said.

'You see, guilt only comes when we have been selfish. It does not matter what that selfishness is about. It could be sex, or it could be anything else. When you take the New York City subway, for instance, and rush ahead of an elderly person to take a seat, could you possibly feel good about it? Whenever self is predominant, you feel guilty. But when the opposite is the case, when your attitude is altruistic, you find a mystical joy bubbling up in your heart. Altruism is natural. When the dog barks to warn the sheep against the wolf, is it not an act of altruism?

'To take advantage of others, to turn another person into an object for the sake of one's own pleasure produces guilt. Compare this situation, if you will, to a devotee who lovingly worships the statue of a goddess. Love can turn a mere object into a worshippable goddess. That is the choice: convert an object into a goddess or convert a goddess into an object! One is selfless, and the other is selfish. One is ennobling, while the other leads to guilt. Do you want to know the secret of transformation? It is only by ennobling others that we ourselves become ennobled. To degrade another person is to degrade one's own self. And to ennoble another person doesn't mean that you are helping them become ennobled. It means that you recognize their innate nobility and revere that. We can pray all day and night for transformation, but it will not come until we approach others with respect, dignity, and a holy reverence.'

'You said that the end result of kama-based desires is a feeling of passion,' I said. 'What is passion?'

'It is to be fixated on one thing,' said Daaji. 'Let us compare two words: passion and compassion. In passion, you are fixated on possessing the person who is the object of your desire. You are more concerned with your own satisfaction than with the other person's feelings. In compassion, on the other hand, you sacrifice yourself for the sake of the other. Passion leads to guilt, but in compassion, you become ennobled. You become joyful. Do you want to know how to attract grace? Be joyful. That is the prescription. What can grace achieve? A single downpour of grace can accomplish what a thousand transmissions can never do, what a thousand blessings can never achieve. So be compassionate, and you will be joyful. Be joyful, and grace will rain down upon you.

'When you are loving, caring, and compassionate with others, you are not trying to get anything from them. You do not manipulate others. You see, the reason that most people like to receive is because they feel incomplete. But though they receive and receive, they are never complete. Wholeness only comes by giving, and the only real gift is of one's own self. So give of yourself. Then you will find that you are receiving much more than you could ever possibly give. *How to give all of this away?* you will wonder. You cannot. You can only continue to give.

'However, generosity of heart does not only mean giving. It is not only about helping others. Real generosity is to accept others' opinions and differences without any vengeful feelings.

'This brings us to dharma, which is the next

category of desire. Actually, I do not feel that dharma should have any connection to desire. Dharma's literal meaning is "that which upholds". That which upholds what? That which upholds righteousness. And we are the ones who must uphold it! To wish for dharma is weakness. To pray for dharma is like praying that you don't rob someone's house. It's easy—just don't do it! If you want dharma in your life—if you want truth and goodness and love—you must be the first one to uphold it. If not you, then who else? So there is no use wishing for dharma. There is no use waiting for dharma. There is no use praying for dharma. You have to be its embodiment. This is dharma's dictate: love all and hurt none. It is also the heart's very nature. You see, we have to cultivate a heart-based understanding of dharma. Too often, our sense of dharma is rooted in our ideologies. The heart's nature is universal, but ideologies are limited. They are the result of our cultures, of our religions, of so many other things. These varying ideologies give rise to differences, dislike, and even hatred. Such impressions take hold at point C, where they petrify into prejudice, which Babuji described as the enemy of spirituality.

'In the Indian tradition, divine personalities

known as avatars are thought to descend in order to restore dharma, in times of intense degradation. Should such a thing really be necessary? Upholding dharma is always something that we would rather thrust onto someone else's shoulders. If we had done our duty to uphold it on our own—without expecting the Lord to descend—we would have saved him a lot of trouble!

'And when we don't uphold dharma? It is not as if we are punished. Rather, we punish ourselves. We bear that burden of guilt. Guilt has a special location in the human frame, which we spoke about earlier. It sinks to point D, where it weighs us down. Our hearts close, and our spiritual expansion is arrested. So we must avoid doing *anything* that will make us feel guilty. There is no external moral authority. The conscience is the only real judge. But the conscience is also stricter than any external judge, and it has the power to punish us far more severely.

'Moksha is the next category of desire for which people strive and pray. In India's religious traditions, moksha generally refers to the state of liberation from the cycle of death and rebirth, and it is often hailed as the highest goal of life. In fact, moksha is a comparatively minor achievement. There is much, much more beyond it.

'Compare the wish for moksha, an emancipated existence in the realm of liberated souls, to the wish to be financially independent, a carefree worldly existence. Are the two wishes so different from one another? In both cases, you seek freedom—a freedom that comes with a change in your circumstances.'

'So the desire for material wealth and the desire for spiritual liberation are similar?' I asked.

'They both create vibrations at point A,' said Daaji. 'Thus, the desire for liberation is counterproductive. It weighs us down, rather than lightening our heavy load. The desire for moksha represents an escapist urge, based upon our negative experiences with the world. For instance, if you eat at a restaurant and the food upsets your stomach, you will probably never want to go there again. Similarly, when we get fed up with the world, we start to become averse to it. Then, you are like a prisoner who wants to break free from his cell. It is not a positive aspiration.

'We also pray for moksha because we think that this liberated state will free us from our slavery to the other three categories of desire. It doesn't. There are many persons amongst us who have already qualified for liberation, yet they still hanker after artha, kama, and dharma. And they also pray for them. Wouldn't it be better to pray for contentment? But if you meditate, why would you need to pray for contentment? It comes by itself!

'And when you are content—when you are already a saint and have no desire for dharma, kama, artha, or moksha—then what will you pray for?'

Daaji paused.

'Whereas you used to pray for yourself, *you now start praying for others.* Of course, this does not mean that you should wait till you become a saint! Even now, you should pray for others. It is not as if prayer can be diluted with the addition of more and more beneficiaries. Rather, it will create an even bigger wave.

'On the other hand,' he said, 'the notion that you can include others in a selfish prayer is contradictory. Suppose that there is a flood in your area. Your heart says, "Please, God, keep my house from flooding," but while praying, you amend that sentiment and say, "Please, God, keep our *neighbourhood* from flooding!" Now, you're confusing God. Your words say one thing, but your heart tells a different story. Is it possible to make up for a selfish prayer by including your neighbours in it? I don't think so. The wrong key can never open the right door! Altruism cannot be an afterthought. It must be your original intention.

'In prayer, our intentions speak much louder than our words. It is your duty to pray for others, no doubt, but without love, duty is always a burden. Your friend asks you for a favour, and though you say yes, you curse him under your breath. Let's take another example. When you dislike your work, it feels like slave labour, and you are resentful. "Why must I have such a hard job?" you fume. On the other hand, when you love what you're doing, it doesn't feel like work at all. In fact, you may be working very hard, but it doesn't feel that way. Hours may pass, but you don't notice the passage of time. When love is present, the idea of duty vanishes, the idea of work vanishes. When we love, we fulfill our duties in the most natural way, without ever feeling their burden. Duty without love makes us slaves, but love frees us. It is the secret to effortless action. It is the foundation, not only of prayer, but of all our acts.'

'How do we convert our self-centered intentions into selfless intentions?' I asked.

'Become selfless,' he replied with a chuckle. 'You see, when the heart is closed, you love only yourself, and your actions are self-serving. When your heart starts to open, you start thinking of your nearest and dearest ones. As your heart continues to open, the circumference of your love expands proportionately. When your heart is infinitely open—when it has no doors, no walls—its love flows throughout the infinite universe. Then, you start to feel that the universe belongs to you—but also that you belong to it. Instead of always thinking of *I*, you now start to think of *we*.

'So let us renounce selfish prayer for once and for all. In fact, rather than praying for oneself and then including others as an afterthought, why not reverse the equation? Let your real intention be for others and include yourself as a mere afterthought.

'However, you will soon find that you do not enjoy including yourself, even as an afterthought. The remembrance of self always deflates the prayer, you see. The whole thing just collapses. When you have faith, why do you need to remind God of your troubles? And if you don't have faith, then why pray at all? Acceptance is the noblest path. You know, both of my gurus were often ill. I think that, with their immense capacity, they could easily have cured themselves in an instant. However, their spiritual dimension did not allow for such things.

Instead, they preferred to accept the situation as it was, with cheer and with gratitude.'

Then, with a sparkle in his eye, he added, 'This does not mean that you should accept your own imperfections!'

'A minute ago, you were speaking about open hearts, but can you tell me what that really means?' I asked.

'Think of a closed heart,' he said. 'Then you will understand.'

'All right,' I said. 'I take your point, but I would still like you to explain it a little bit, if you don't mind.'

'I'll tell you a story,' said Daaji. 'Every morning, as the sun got ready to rise, his personal assistant would come, and along with his coffee, he would present the sun with a list of names of those people whom the sun should not forget to shine upon.

"Sir, this man in Argentina very much needs your warmth. Make sure you remember to shine on him," and "Sir, there is a little girl in China who is so delightful. Make sure you remember her, too."

'One day, after a long day of shining, the sun was about to set, when his assistant ran up to him.

"Sir, you cannot set now! You have not completed your work for the day."

"What do you mean?" asked the sun. "I shone all day long, just as I do every day. Now I am tired and want to rest."

"Do you remember that man in Argentina I mentioned this morning?" asked the sun's assistant.

"Yes, of course I remember," said the sun.

"But he remained in the dark all day long. You did not shine on him as you'd promised," said the assistant.

'The sun ruminated for a moment and said, "My dear, it is my nature to shine for one and all, and I have done so. Tell me, what can I do if this man shuts himself indoors all day long with the curtains drawn?"

'An open heart is like the sun that shines for one and all. It can do nothing but radiate its love. From the open heart, love flows indiscriminately. However, we cannot really say that the heart loves. Rather, an open heart is love itself, and anyone who steps out into its rays feels that they are being loved. And what is a closed heart? It is like the man who shut himself indoors all day long.

'An open heart is a giving heart, but it is a receiving heart as well. In this sense, a heart that is open is a heart that is humble.'

'I don't follow,' I said.

'Any egotist can give, but it takes a humble person to receive,' Daaji said.

Pulling a coin from his pocket, he handed it to me. As he did so, he asked, 'Do you see the position of your hand?' It was open, palm facing upward.

'We associate this pose with asking,' he said. 'Prayer is to ask for higher help. Whether you ask for yourself or for others, asking always requires humility, which is what allows us to pray in the first place.

'Conversely, if I were to think of myself as the Giver, as the Infinite Source, then nobody in the world could help me. Even God could not help me. I must have the humility to realize that no matter what I may give to others, none of it has originated with me. If I give someone a dollar, I must also have received it from somewhere, no?'

'Can I keep the coin?' I asked. Daaji chuckled.

'You're a joker!' he said.

Giving the coin back, I said, 'Okay, this is for the wisdom.'

'Oh, it's worth so little?' he bantered. 'Well anyway, I don't charge anything, so you keep it!'

'In that case, I'll ask you another question,' I said. 'How do we know the best thing to pray for in any given situation?'

'This is a question that only the intellect can ask,' he replied, 'and unfortunately, there is no answer with which to satisfy it. Prayer emerges automatically from a heart that loves, so only a loving heart can answer this question. The rational mind can never know the answer.

'You must have heard that famous Chinese folktale about the farmer and his neighbour,' Daaji said.

I had not, and asked him to relate the story.

'Long ago, there was a very wise farmer,' he began. 'One day, his horse ran away. When his neighbour offered his condolences, the farmer simply said, "Who knows what is good and what is bad?" The next day, the horse returned along with an entire herd of wild horses. This time, the neighbour congratulated the farmer, but again, the farmer replied, "Who knows what is good and what is bad?" The farmer's son tried to tame one of the wild horses. It threw him, and the farmer's son broke his leg. The neighbour again offered his condolences. Again, the farmer replied, "Who knows what is good and what is bad?"

'Soon afterward, war broke out with a neighbouring territory. Some military officers came to draft the farmer's son into the fight, but upon their arrival they found him incapacitated with his broken leg. In the ensuing war, many young men from the farmer's village were killed, but the farmer's son survived due to his broken leg.

'Imagine if the farmer had prayed for his son to be protected from being injured by the wild horses. If that prayer had been answered, he could have become a casualty of war.

'We never know what will turn out for the best or for the worst. We could only know it if we already knew the outcome, but in that case, why would we need to pray?

'During periods of armed conflict, everybody prays. But if every faction is praying for victory, to whom will God respond? The war itself hurts Him. After all, His children are fighting! It is foolishness that makes us pray for such things.' Daaji shook his head sadly, and said, 'It only shows how little we know of God.

'Even our altruistic prayers can easily go wrong,' he continued. 'Suppose, for example, that you decide to pray for a person's fear to be removed. It's a noble thing, right? Well, it certainly looks great on the surface, but it may be that some amount of fear was necessary in that particular case. What would happen if God were to bestow fearlessness upon a bandit or limitless courage upon a corrupt official in a high position? They would only become more brazen, no? In such cases, fearlessness would be counterproductive. My father used to say that if you were to bestow wealth upon a person who has no character, who lacks a moral compass, the wealth would only destroy him. There are many examples of this in our society, where those born into extreme privilege find themselves on life's difficult roads. We can never know the direction in which such things will take our near and dear ones.'

'So how do we know what to pray for?' I asked.

'When your heart is sensitized, it becomes responsive to the true needs of others. Then, your prayers will always be in natural accordance with that need.'

'All right, then how do you sensitize your heart?' I pressed.

'Do you really want to?' he said. 'When you already have so many pains and troubles of your own, do you really want to share in the pains and troubles of others? The first prerequisite of sensitivity is the willingness to do just that. The knowledge of another person's suffering cannot rise to your awareness until you are able to tolerate that suffering. Secondly, what is the point of your being aware of the plight of others? Suppose that someone hacks into your bank account. Now, they are aware of your financial situation, but do you really think that they have your best interests at heart?'

'Of course not,' I said.

'There's no good reason for me to know about your finances unless my intent is to help you, right? Similarly, there is no need to become sensitive to others unless you are going to use that sensitivity for their betterment. Only love can make this possible, and when there is love, tolerance will also be present. With these two qualities, your heart will intuit your prayers in the most natural way. It is when we lack these qualities that we become confused about what we should pray for.

'However, if you have the ability to physically help someone, don't be content to just sit back and pray. Instead, do something! Lend a helping hand. Chariji used to say that prayer is the first means of the weak and the last means of the strong. If you can do nothing, then by all means, pray. But if you can feed someone, do it. If you can house someone, do it. It is your human obligation to try to solve circumstances before you pray for them. Of course, if you do not have enough to feed your own family, then it cannot be correct to feed someone else's family. You must always fulfill your own duties first.'

'This reminds me of the proverb "Charity begins at home,"' I said.

'Yes,' said Daaji. 'It is sad that we cannot always do very much to alleviate suffering. Although we may want to help everybody in this world, we simply do not have the personal resources to do so. The least you can do for a suffering person is to spend time with him. Commiserate with him. Sit next to him. You may say nothing; you may do nothing. You are simply there. Your very presence is impactful, you see. Because of it, your friend perceives that "Now, my help is here", and this gives him strength.'

Connecting through Prayer

'What is the best way to pray?' I asked.

'Between the singer who hits every note and the singer who means every note, we prefer the latter, don't we?'

'Yes,' I agreed.

'And when an artist has moved you, you easily forgive their wrong note or their unpolished brushstroke,' he said. 'Only sincerity can touch the human heart. If a person were to say, "I love you" in angry tones, would we feel moved?

'In prayer too, it is feeling and sincerity that count. There's a nice story that comes to mind. An ordinary cowherd was looking after his cows and buffalos. Every night, he prayed to the Lord, and said, "If you come join me, I'll protect you from the heat by letting you sit in the shade of my favourite tree. I'll give you a bath. And whenever you like, I'll scratch your back." This prayer was heard over and over again by a Brahmin, a priest, who lived next door to the farmer. One day, the Brahmin said, "What sort of prayer is this? You're going to give a bath to God? You're going to scratch his back? This is nonsense." So the farmer humbly said, "You teach me." The Brahmin agreed and taught him some Sanskrit *shlokas,* or verses.

'The next day, the farmer forgot the words. "Please teach me again," he said. "I forgot what you taught me." The Brahmin taught him again, but the farmer forgot them again. This process repeated itself a few times. In the end, the farmer was confused and disheartened.

'Then, God came to the Brahmin in a dream one night and said, "Look, you have really spoiled this fellow's life. His prayer was the best prayer." He had expressed himself, you see. He said, "This is what I'm going to do with you. It's all that I know." A Sanskrit thing, you forget. You don't even understand the meaning of it. It's not that we're decrying the value of the ancient shlokas. They're wonderful. But you have to understand them. A prayer has to have meaning to you. Otherwise, you are like a parrot.

'Words are not feeling—they are only depictions of feeling. A prayer offered by rote is only a husk of a feeling. As such, it remains hollow. An efficacious prayer is one in which the words reverberate with the heart's feeling. Yet, when the heart reverberates with feeling, is there any need for words?

'It is only through silence that we commune with the inner Being. In such silence, even our thoughts are mute.'

'I can understand silent prayer,' I said, 'but a prayer without thoughts?'

'The act of prayer must evolve into a prayerful inner state,' said Daaji. 'For instance, have you observed the interactions of a couple who have been married for decades? A single glance speaks volumes, and hardly any words need to be spoken. Over the years, they have transcended the need for communication and entered into a state of communion with one another. The less two people understand of one another, the more they need to communicate. When a couple is newly married, a lot of communication is required. The more they understand of one another, the subtler their communication becomes, and when they know each other deeply, communication becomes redundant.

'Similarly, in our attempt to reconnect with our Origin, we begin with formal prayer. Prayer is only the first step. It must mature into prayerfulness. For example, it is common to pray before eating, but if after that prayer is completed, you attack your food like a wolf, what happens to the prayerful mood that you have just created? Without a prayerful inner state, prayer is only an artifice. It is absurd.

'Often, we teach children to write by giving them stencils of the letters of the alphabet. By tracing the letters, they learn how to write on their own. Similarly, formal prayer must evolve into prayerfulness. Thereafter, formal prayer becomes unnecessary and redundant. If we do not graduate into prayerfulness, we are like adults who still rely upon stencils to write the alphabet.

'This inner state is unique. It has no external face or any external principles to be followed, meaning rituals. The moment you make prayer a ritual, it loses its importance.

'However, prayerfulness is just another beginning. Its purpose is to take us beyond, to take us to yet another level.'

'What lies beyond prayerfulness?' I asked him.

'Oneness,' said Daaji. 'Duality is intrinsic to prayer. In prayer, there are always two: a person in need and the personality whose help is needed. I offer prayer, and the Great Being is supposed to listen to me and answer my prayers. Without this duality, who would offer prayer, and who would receive it? The distinction between the divine presence and me still remains. There are still two. There is still a relationship. Through meditation, on the other hand, we progressively enter into a state of oneness with the divine presence within. We transcend relationship.

'With prayer alone, the possibility of union is rather far-fetched. We remain what we are, and the Source remains what it is.'

'Then what role does prayer have to play?' I asked.

'It helps us become heartfully cognizant of that divine principle with which we intend to merge,' said Daaji. 'Prayer should be offered in such a way that it transforms into meditation. Truly, it is an eruption of the heart, highlighting the pang of separation from the Beloved. "I can bear this no longer," it says. I am reminded of one couplet from my childhood: "O Lord, please visit my little hut at least once. I will treat you so nicely, so lovingly, that you will forget your heavenly abode." Prayer is, in a way, an inner cry where pearls of tears slowly flow down the face and beautify the heart's inner complexities. This pang of the heart serves to keep us glued to the cherished object, and eventually, like a river flowing into the sea, prayerfulness resolves in meditative togetherness with the Source.'

The Heartfulness Prayer

We offer the Heartfulness prayer once before our daily meditation and again just before we go to sleep at the end of our day. If offered in the right spirit, this silent prayer creates a unique inner state. In my early days of practising Heartfulness, I treated the prayer almost as a formality. Because of this, my heart never looked forward to it. Eventually, I stopped it altogether. One evening, however, I felt particularly drawn to its words, and I offered the prayer with all my heart. Immediately, my inner spiritual condition changed. That night, my sleep was more like deep meditation than regular sleep. When I woke up in the morning, my inner state was unique. Furthermore, my meditation had a special quality about it, which had previously been absent. As a result of this experience, I stopped ignoring the prayer. Instead, it became a fundamental part of my life. Even now, I continue to discover it on a daily basis.

> O Master, Thou art the real goal of human life.
> We are yet but slaves of wishes, putting bar to
> our advancement.
> Thou art the only God and power to bring us
> up to that stage.

'What is the purpose of offering prayer before we sleep?' I asked.

'It is the best way to create a prayerful *waking* state,' said Daaji. 'The purpose of prayer is to reestablish our connection with the Divine. But prayerfulness is something different. Prayerfulness dawns when we already feel the divine presence. Then we feel like bowing our heads, and we wish to melt away in that divine ocean.

'We experience that magnetic presence when we turn toward the Divine with body, mind, and soul. This total orientation to the Divine cannot be manufactured with the conscious mind. In the daytime, when we are fully awake, the intellect tends to dominate our consciousness. The intellect has its purpose, but it is not useful for creating a prayerful inner state.

'During the period between wakefulness and sleep, however, there is a convergence between the conscious and subconscious states. The curtain is temporarily lifted, and now the two can meet. At this moment, our brainwaves fall into a pattern known by modern scientists as the alpha state. While in the alpha state, we enter into a kind of inner reverie, in which we become highly susceptible to suggestions. Now, we can deliberately seed the subconscious with prayerful thoughts. These thoughts put down roots and grow in the fertile ground of the subconscious. Just as seeds germinate underground, where they are hidden from sight, our prayers germinate and grow in the obscurity of our subconscious, before bursting forth into our wakeful awareness. In this way, we can seed prayers into the subconscious and harvest a prayerful waking state.

'But we must offer the prayer with feeling. The subconscious only knows the language of feeling, you see. You may sow the subconscious with empty words, but those are like dead seeds that can never germinate. At bedtime, we are often too sleepy to rouse ourselves with true feeling. So, we can practise offering the prayer during the day, while still alert. Create that feeling while you are alert. Then, when you offer it again at bedtime, the very act of praying will revive your earlier state.

'During the daytime, when the intellect is in full swing, we can also understand the meaning of the prayer from another perspective. In fact, I wish for every newcomer to this practice—and even seasoned practitioners—to take a day or two and try to understand the true significance and meaning of the prayer. There is more to this prayer than its wording suggests. Then, see what is hidden behind the meaning you discover. Meditate over it again and again. Take the first line, the second line, the third line, and ruminate over every word. Do not rush! New dimensions will open up every time.

'Prayer's purpose is to transform you. People usually think that transformation comes from above, as a result of having prayed. But it is the offering of the prayer that transforms us, rather than its response. This transformation happens in the very moment that we pray. True prayer is its own answer, you see.

'To forge an intimate connection with your

Maker, your heart must be innocent and pure. "Be ye like little children," said Lord Christ. Guilt is utterly destructive. It is like lead in the heart. The guilty heart hides itself from the Divine, isolating itself in its self-made prison. In that case, how will we bathe in the restorative rays of the Source? There is no question of whether we will be received and accepted by God. Can a mother withhold her love and forgiveness? Rather, it is we who cannot accept or forgive ourselves. Repentance is not a ritual. Self-forgiveness only comes when our hearts repent for our mistakes. To cry your heart out is worth a thousand prayers for forgiveness. Tears are the sign of sincerity—even when our hearts are light and happy.'

'What if we don't feel guilty about anything?' I asked.

'Then congratulations,' he laughed. 'You must be a saint. But, even a saint finds room for improvement. *Especially* the saint, in fact, because she is so humble that she always finds herself to be at fault, even when she really is not. As we become more receptive to the voice of the conscience, we find that it holds us accountable for smaller and smaller matters. Even at the subtlest hint of a wrong thought, we find that the conscience pricks.

So at night, scan your heart and see where your conscience is pricking you. See where you feel uncomfortable and find out the reason. Without such introspection, there is no possibility of improvement.

'On the other hand, the notion of self-improvement is paradoxical. When there is 'self,' there is no improvement. If you introspect with ego, thinking that *I will correct myself,* it cannot work. Too much of your "I" is present. In prayer, on the other hand, your heart simply droops in surrender, and you leave everything to the higher Being, saying, "Please, let thy will be done." What is needed is a mixture of introspection and surrender—a friendly pact between you and God. Through prayerful introspection, you discover your defects, but rather than resolving to correct them yourself, you relinquish yourself and invoke higher help.

'Of course, it would be better to avoid making mistakes day after day, hour after hour! It is said that a fool recognizes a mistake in retrospect, and an intelligent person recognizes it during the act, but a wise person knows beforehand and avoids it.'

'How can we know beforehand?' I asked.

'With prayerful alertness,' he replied.

'To what?' I asked.

'To the signals that emanate from your own heart and guide you from within,' he said. 'If you maintain this attitude throughout your daily affairs, wisdom will positively flourish.

'When you are ready to offer prayer, do so with a humble heart—a heart full of love.

'Sit up, gently close your eyes, and relax. Repeat the prayer mentally twice or thrice, lingering over every word and phrase so that you are able to sense its meaning as deeply as you can. Meditate over this meaning and allow yourself to get lost, or absorbed, in this prayerful meditation. When you feel ready, go straight to sleep.

'After you finish the prayer, make sure that you take care to preserve the condition that you have just created. Don't just plop your head on the pillow. Move slowly. Sink gradually into the reclining pose. Don't start thinking about your day or your plans for tomorrow. The condition that you have just created must be allowed to continue percolating within you as you drift off.'

'So this prayer becomes a meditation,' I said.

'It is a prayer-meditation that creates a meditatively prayerful state,' he replied. 'Babuji received this prayer in the form of vibrations, which he experienced as feelings and then translated into words. Our job is to reverse the process. We translate these words back into the feelings that constitute their essence, by which they arrive at the Source from where they originated. By meditating upon its words, we discover its deeper essence. This uplifts our consciousness. When we go to sleep in this consciousness, our sleep gets transformed into a very special state known as yoganidra, or yogic sleep.'

'What is yoganidra?' I asked.

'There are people who sleep so deeply that even if you throw water on them, they will not wake up,' said Daaji. 'For others, your mere presence in the room wakes them up. Generally, we can identify a spectrum between sound sleep and light sleep. In yoganidra, our consciousness expands in an omnidirectional manner. While moving toward deep sleep, it simultaneously expands toward wakeful awareness. As a result, we are in both states simultaneously. While sleeping deeply, we are also profoundly awake. So in yoganidra, we are able to expand consciousness, rather than deriving only physical and mental rest.

'But much more happens in this state, in fact. A yogi can work in other locations, in other dimensions, in other times. Astral travel also takes place, where the physical form does not limit your work. Yoganidra is the best situation for all this to occur, but this is a matter for personal experience, rather than for discussion. Let us now focus on what is fathomable, according to the level of evolution that we all share. Essentially, let us realize that the yoganidra state prepares you to soar higher into the sky of superconsciousness during morning meditation.'

'How does it do that?' I asked.

'The quality of any meditation is largely determined by our attitude, or mood. Moods develop gradually and wane gradually. You cannot snap your fingers and command a meditative mood to arise at that moment of need. It must already be in you. But if you meditate first thing in the morning, when will that mood have had a chance to develop? It must develop during sleep.'

'And for this, we must plant the right seed at bedtime,' I said.

'Yes,' said Daaji. 'The bedtime prayer triggers a prayerful consciousness, filled with anticipation to unite with the Source. This anticipation swells throughout the night, and by morning, we approach our meditation with an inner joy that draws us deeper into the Source.'

'At night we pray, and then we go to sleep,' I said. 'In the morning we also pray, but then we meditate instead. What determines whether we go to sleep or go into meditation?'

'Our subliminal intention,' said Daaji. 'When we offer this prayer in the morning, just before we meditate, we don't repeat it two to three times as we do at night. We offer it only once and start to meditate.'

'Why?' I asked.

'If you offer the prayer in the right spirit at bedtime, that prayerful state will still be with you in the morning. Even if it's not, all you will require is a brief reminder. Like a horse that runs at the mere shadow of the whip, our inner state gets enlivened with a single offering of prayer. To soar into the skies of superconsciousness now becomes a child's play.'

PRAYER

- Sit comfortably and gently close your eyes.
- In the morning:
- Slowly and silently, offer the prayer once before you begin meditation.
- At bedtime:
- Silently repeat the prayer a few times, pausing in between. Meditate for ten to fifteen minutes over the true meaning of the words. Feel them resonate in your heart, rather than trying to understand them intellectually. Let the meaning surface from within. Try to get lost in the feeling beyond the words.

O Master! Thou art the real goal of human life.
We are yet but slaves of wishes, putting bar to our advancement.
Thou art the only God and power to bring us up to that stage.

Part Three

The Guru

6

The Role of the Guru

THROUGHOUT MY CONVERSATIONS with Daaji, he often made mention of his two gurus, Babuji and Chariji. However, most of these references were in passing, and I felt that without a deeper examination of the role of the guru, our discussions would be incomplete.

'Your gurus obviously had an enormous impact on your life,' I said. 'Would you say that it is necessary to have a guru in order to evolve spiritually?'

'First, let us understand what a guru is,' said Daaji. 'Then, you decide whether or not he is necessary!'

'Okay,' I said, 'then what is a guru?'

'That's also up to you!' he replied. 'At what level

do you accept him? To some, having a guru is a mere formality. To others, the guru is a teacher. To some people, he is the teaching itself—its embodied, living example. And then, there are those people for whom the guru is its very essence. Really, the guru is all of these.

'Teaching is the guru's lowest level. It is his lowest function. Teaching is limited because if a person does not truly crave divine knowledge, no teacher can make them learn. If they do crave it, then they will find hints everywhere, and teaching will become redundant.

'Also, the knowledge we receive through teaching is always secondhand knowledge. Secondhand knowledge doesn't enlighten us very much. It is better to observe and experience something for yourself. Also, you always check a guru's words against your own heart. If your heart agrees with them, you say, "Yes, the guru is correct." If your heart says no, then you ignore the guru. So who is the real guru—the one who gives you lessons or your own heart?'

'So the guru's purpose is not really to teach,' I said.

'If the guru has any teaching at all, it is their example,' said Daaji. 'Yet, what do we see when we observe the guru? I'm reminded of something that Babuji once said: "Many come to see me, but nobody really sees me." Often, people try to copy the guru's example, but they miss his essence. They miss the very thing that makes the guru worth copying. Instead, they only mime the guru's actions, dress, or mannerisms. Thus, the real thing eludes them. They miss out on the guru's essential nature.

'This is not their fault. In order to assess anything and be conclusive about it, we must be subtler than the object under assessment. That is why the guru consistently eludes the student. His degree of subtlety prevents us from truly observing him. At most, we see a refined person who occasionally says something wise. The very subtlest thing is the Ultimate itself. So how can it ever be observed, and how can we ever conclude anything about it?

'But through spiritual practice, we become subtler, too. Now, we start to grasp more of what the guru actually is. And to the extent that we can grasp the guru, we can pick up on things. As I said already, he will rarely teach us anything. We have to pick it up on our own.

'Really, the guru does nothing at all. Nor does

he have to. Can night exist in the presence of the sun? The sun rises, and darkness simply retreats. The sun does nothing to make the darkness retreat. Its nature is to be as it is. Similarly, the guru. The literal meaning of the word guru is "dispeller of darkness". But, like the sun, the guru does nothing to dispel the darkness. He simply is as he is.

'The moment that the bud comes into contact with the sun's rays, it slowly starts to open up. Did the sun actually do anything to make this happen? Did the bud? It just happens.

'So the guru does nothing—it is his *presence* that does everything. And his presence only works when the aspirant's heart is ready to flower. Trying to force open a bud would only destroy it. If the guru were to act upon us, it would be an imposition. It would be destructive. So the guru will not do it.'

'But the guru does clean us and transmit to us,' I said.

'No,' said Daaji. 'It is because of the guru's presence that we become clean. It is because of his presence that we receive transmission. The guru does nothing at all. But to become what he is, he had to work hard on himself, just as we have to work hard on ourselves. We have to practise!

Through practice, we prepare our hearts so that they draw everything out of the guru. That is why we meditate, clean, and offer prayer, day after day. Without our work, the guru's presence in our lives goes to waste.'

'So our personal work is the catalyst,' I said.

'Yes,' said Daaji. 'Practice is essential. You can meet the guru every day, you can eat your meals with him and rub shoulders with him, but if your heart isn't prepared, it won't help you one little bit.

'But if your heart *is* prepared, then why would you need to meet the guru so often? The guru works from afar. Of course, he does not really work, but work happens through him. And you need not be in the guru's physical presence for that work to take place. That is a limitation we set in our own minds. The guru need not know your name. He need not be familiar with your face. Such conscious knowledge is totally unnecessary for his work. The guru need not even be aware that he is working on you because spiritual work proceeds automatically from his heart. Your heart has called out, and the guru is nature's response. Thus, the guru-aspirant relationship is an inner one, fanned in the secrecy of the heart.'

'To what extent do we need to personally interact with a guru?' I asked.

'The relationship need not manifest on the human level at all,' said Daaji. 'Nevertheless, it is best to meet your guru once in your life. This doesn't mean that you have to shake hands and have a conversation. But be around him once. If your attitude is right at that time, if you are receptive, something special happens. Your entire spiritual journey is plotted out. Any additional meeting is just a bonus. We needn't follow the guru around, as we see happening so often in India. We should never worship the guru, as so many people do. These people believe that the physical frame of the guru contains the Ultimate Source. His frame does not contain the Source. The Source is nowhere. It can also be anywhere, but the only place that you will ever find it is *within yourself*. The purpose of the external guru is to lead you to the inner one—the divine Self, which guides and inspires us.

'And it must be a living guru—a guru from ages past cannot help you. Can you illuminate a room with a flame that has been extinguished? All that remains is their teachings. It's book knowledge.'

'So we need a living example,' I said.

'Even an example isn't necessary,' said Daaji. 'If you don't meet him very often, of what use can his example be? What we really need is the essence that he infuses in our hearts in the form of transmission.

'Of course, the essence is everywhere because the Source is everywhere! But without a living guru to distill it and focus it on our hearts, we remain blind to it. We remain unaffected by it, and we struggle without end because there is no help.

'Without someone to help us, we have trouble going beyond ourselves, beyond our own limitations. Imagine trying to move a broken-down car by pushing it from the inside. No matter how hard you push, that car will never move. It needs an external push to help it along. The guru is that push. We have been pushing ourselves from the inside for so long. Eventually, we realize that this is a field in which we need guidance in order to progress.'

'How do we find a guru?' I asked.

'The guru is the response to the sincere seeker,' he replied. 'Babuji often said that the true cry of the aspirant brings the master to their door. In some cases, the aspirant is conscious of this inner cry. In other cases, this cry unconscious. And while it is true that the aspirant draws the guru, what is equally true is that the guru selects the aspirant.'

'How so?' I asked.

'In my childhood, I had a number of experiences,' said Daaji. 'Whenever I fell sick, I would have one dream. In this dream, I would see a rider atop a white steed. He was dressed in a white flowing gown, and he had a beautiful white beard. Normally, you forget dreams, but when you have the same dream over and over again, you tend to remember it.'

'How old were you?' I asked.

'It started when I was around four or five, and it came periodically until I was eleven. That last time, I was studying outside, sitting in a cloth beach chair. This was in our village. There, I had this vision once again, and entered into samadhi. I was gone for hours.

'Soon after that last experience, I started feeling an inner pull, a kind of aspiration. I told my family members that I had started to feel something special in my heart. Years later, I would learn that at the time of this experience, Babuji was passing through my area. When I finally met him, years later, I immediately recognized his face. He was the figure in white who had been appearing to me since childhood.'

'So he was already preparing you,' I said.

'The guru prepares all of us far in advance,' said Daaji. 'But at some level, I was conscious of it. Generally, such preparation is unconscious. It takes place in secrecy, unknown to us and anyone else. It's like a seed that germinates underground. Only the sower knows that it is there.

'Wherever Babuji would go, he would transmit. Those who were ready would eventually answer the call. Somehow, we all made our way to him on our own. In the 1940s, he toured India by train. In certain places, he would stop and hire a rickshaw to take him around the city. Sitting in the back, he would transmit everywhere he went. When he was satisfied that the area had been seeded with spiritual potential to the desired extent, he would take the train elsewhere and repeat the process. Babuji continued this seeding throughout his life, though later on he would do it without leaving his house.'

'So is it that the guru prepares us or that our hearts call the guru?' I asked.

'His very existence is a response to the collective inner need,' said Daaji. 'Due to his presence, some people awaken to that need. Their hearts cry out. Spiritual aspiration is present in all, but it in many cases it is dormant. Sometimes, it only takes a touch of transmission, and you become awakened to your deeper purpose. So, the guru transmits and transmits. That transmission is like an invitation. If we are responsive, we find our way to the guru. He cannot force us to come. Your heart must permit it. The guru can never go against your heart. No matter how great a guru he may be, the unwilling heart deflects his work.

'That is why it is not possible to enforce inner change. There must be willingness on the part of the aspirant. Only then can the guru's work bear fruit. In the relationship between the aspirant and a capable guru, the aspirant is the deciding factor—never the guru. A guru may be great, he may be powerful, but he can never impose that power upon us.

'There are a number of unfortunate examples where charlatans pose as gurus and exert power over others for the sake of personal profit or to satisfy their own egos. That is one reason why blind faith is dangerous. We should only put our full faith in someone when they have already proved themselves to be trustworthy and capable. Faith only comes when we see a pattern of results—never before. It should never be blind.'

'But how do you recognize a guru in the first place?' I asked.

'There are no outward signs,' said Daaji. 'A true guru will not show off. You can know a zebra by its stripes and a leopard by its spots. But a guru? Anyone can put on robes and grow a beard. Such external features are meaningless and therefore unnecessary as well. A guru may be tall, or he may be short. His appearance may be regal or nondescript. He may be well educated or even illiterate. He may be articulate. He may fumble upon his words. He may be wealthy, or he may be a pauper. We learn nothing from the guru's outer attributes. The only deciding factor is the guru's inner spiritual dimension.

'But how to determine this? If you were able to comprehend the guru's inner state, you might not even need a guru!'

'Then what is the way to test him?' I asked.

'When your soul in its wisdom finds the person who is right, you will feel peace and calmness in your heart,' said Daaji. 'It may come immediately after starting your spiritual practice, or it may come after some time, but it will come. When this is the case, know for sure that this is the one who can guide you.'

'For how long do we need to practise before we find this peace and calmness?' I asked.

'Well, it depends on you,' he said. 'In my very first sitting, I knew that I had found what I was looking for. For others, it can take a few weeks or a few months. You see, some people need time to be convinced by their own experience.'

'And how can you tell if it's the wrong person?' I asked.

'Your heart will start doubting,' said Daaji. 'Of course, the mind will always have a few doubts. Its nature is to question things. But when your heart is restless and heavy with doubt, know that this person is not for you.

'Conversely, when your heart is satisfied, then don't go on entertaining mental doubts forever. Now, it's time to settle down in your practice and work on yourself.

'But you always have the right to leave your guru if you are unsatisfied. There should be no trepidation about parting ways with any guru. The guru has no right to expect discipleship. He has no right to be followed.

'Aspirants always retain the right to sever their connection with a guru. For the guru's part, he should always assist the aspirant to find someone better than himself if he is unable to take the aspirant any further on the spiritual journey.

'In 1961, one seeker came to Babuji. This seeker already had a guru—a Swamiji, as he called him. However, in Babuji's presence, he had a better experience. So he wrote a letter to Babuji saying that had a problem. He wanted to take Babuji as his guru, but at the same time, he didn't want to betray his Swamiji. I have Babuji's reply to that letter.'

Daaji disappeared into his bedroom and returned a minute later.

'I'll read you one paragraph from Babuji's reply,' he said. 'Babuji writes: "As far as I am concerned, please consider me as your servant, keeping the house clean by sweeping out the garbage. Consider me as the servant, and Swamiji as the Master. I have no hesitation in serving you and also wish you to keep paying the wages of this service to Swamiji."

'Also,' Daaji continued, 'in my personal experiences with Babuji, I never found him to comport himself as if he was a guru, or a master. Rather, he seemed to regard himself as someone who was completely insignificant.

'I'm reminded of one instance when a big government official came to visit him. The official got off the train at Shahjahanpur [the city in which Babuji lived] and found a man there to receive him. Without a word, the official handed over his luggage and the two of them proceeded by rickshaw to Babuji's house. Now, this official was rather large, and he had a lot of luggage too, so there was not enough room on the seat for the two of them. So, the official sat on the seat, and the other man sat on the rickshaw's floor. When they arrived at Babuji's house, the man took the official's luggage and brought it to his room. Later, the official went to pay his respects to Babuji. There, he received the shock of his life. He saw this same little man sitting in Babuji's chair. Now it dawned on him that Babuji had personally received him at the station! He had taken Babuji for a servant.

'You know, there is one Sanskrit word: *mahatma.* Maha means "great", and atma means "soul", so mahatma means "great soul". Often, the term is applied honorifically. In some cases, it is even self-applied! Well, Babuji disliked this word very much. He said that a true mahatma has no greatness, but rather, is one who is totally insignificant—to himself, to the world, and to everything. He is absolutely humble. If you ever think that you have become great, you're digging your own grave. A true mahatma is one who claims nothing, who promises nothing, who has *become* nothing. But such figures are often neglected in favour of disingenuous or deluded gurus who wield charm, charisma, and petty miracles to secure disciples for themselves.

'A guru should never even entertain the idea that he is a guru. If this feeling enters into his heart even once, I think he becomes immediately disqualified for the job. Really, a guru should consider himself to be something even less than a servant. But instead, we tend to find so many self-proclaimed gurus. You know, I never heard Chariji refer to himself as anything other than a disciple of Babuji. And Babuji ... he was so humble that the word "I" seemed to confuse him.

'You see, not many really know what a guru is. It seems that people are content to call someone a guru if he simply puts on ocher robes, or if he displays knowledge of ancient texts or speaks wise words. Many gurus don't even give you a practice. They may give you a few exercises, but their work stops there. There is no continuous inner contact. Really, it is like being abandoned by the side of the road! Can such gurus trigger the spiritual journey and keep us moving until we reach the far-off shore? Can they clear away the inner intricacies and complexities that ensnare us and bar further progress? Can they weaken the restless tendencies of the mind and infuse noble qualities in our hearts? Can they remove our samskaric load? There are also many other things that the guru must do in order to ensure our safe arrival at the destination. Ultimately, the guru bears responsibility for the spiritual progress of each aspirant under his care. He must answer for each one of them, both to his own guru and to nature itself. I think that nature will impose a heavy penalty on any guru who is unable or unwilling to fulfill these duties. It is better to have no guru at all than to have a useless or malevolent guru.

'And there are also gurus who get jealous if a student excels them. Should a parent ever be jealous of their children? It is every parent's dream to see their child exceed them. Similarly, a true guru will not be satisfied with taking you beyond yourself—he wants to take you beyond *himself*. He wants you to rise to the very pinnacle of evolutionary heights—a pinnacle that keeps getting higher.'

'What do you mean by that?' I asked.

'What was considered the greatest spiritual attainment one thousand years ago cannot compare to today's possibilities. And what is possible today may be nothing compared to tomorrow's possibilities.'

'So spirituality keeps evolving,' I said.

'Yes,' said Daaji. 'In the time of Copernicus, for instance, the idea that the earth revolves around the sun was something new. In those days, it represented the very best of modern scientific understanding. It was cutting edge. Today, every child takes this knowledge for granted. These days, we are fascinated with things like quantum mechanics instead. Does that diminish Copernicus in any way? No! That he knew nothing of Einstein or Hawking does not reduce his stature. In his own time, he was great.

'Similarly, the spiritual elders of the past were great in their own times. But times also change. Today's spiritual giants make new discoveries. Do you think yesterday's luminaries are jealous? Wherever they are, they must be dancing! We also hope for a new generation of spiritual geniuses who will one day exceed those of today.

'Another meaning of the word guru is "great one" or "big one". From something big, things can flow toward us. That means that the guru is a giver. But in today's world, gurus tend to be receivers instead. They like to be worshipped. They like to receive guru *dakshina* [traditional fees]. They want to have attention, they want to be loved, they want to be revered, they want to be followed. A real guru wants none of this. A guru should never be at the receiving end. He never says, "Follow me." Rather, he stays where he is and allows his disciples to go ahead of him. *Let me see how high you can climb,* he thinks. Of course, his vigilant eyes will always be there. He is always protecting. He won't think, *Let him go higher and see if he falls!*

'At the same time, the guru is the biggest obstacle on our spiritual path.'

'Really?' I said.

'Yes, because you keep depending on him for everything,' said Daaji. '"His grace will take care of everything," you say. It's nonsense. His help is there, no doubt, but you've got to prepare yourself. You've got to work hard on yourself.

'Don't think that I'm trying to praise myself, but I moved to the US with twenty dollars in my pocket. My father was always willing to help me, but I didn't look forward to that help. I stood on my own two legs and became successful.

'That's why I often say, "Think that your guru is dead." This means that you should work as if you had no guru. The guru is not the giver of progress, you see. Rather, he is its *catalyst.* Our work attracts his energies. When you take a single step on the path, he takes you one step further. The only difference is that his single footstep can cover infinite realms of consciousness.

'When you practise, a capable guru ensures that your spiritual journey begins as soon as possible, and he continuously ensures that you stay in motion so that your journey continues.

'In whatever stage you may be at present, the guru is busy preparing the ground for the next stage. A guru can even give you the condition of a very high stage, far before you have actually reached it.

'This happened to me in 1982. I was visiting Babuji at his home in Shahjahanpur. One afternoon, I went out to run an errand. When I returned, Babuji looked at me and said, "You should remain in this condition twenty-four hours a day." I had to look inside to understand what he was talking about.

'At that time, I was almost a beginner, but the condition he gave me was something that comes at an extremely advanced stage. Babuji had not actually put me in that advanced stage. I was not ready for it yet, so instead, he gave me the *experience* of that stage. He gave me the quality of that stage without actually putting me there. Really, such things are completely unheard of! A great guru can do magical things, you see.

'Also, there is a certain juncture that comes at each and every stage of the spiritual journey. It is a stage in which seekers tend to get wobbly. They think, *What am I doing messing around with spirituality?* Then, they can disappear. So the guru has to stabilize their emotions at that point and satisfy them with experiences.

'A guru must at least be able to take you to the stage of moksha—liberation. This is an elementary step, and it is barely the beginning of the journey. Really, the guru should be able to bring you to the stage of realization—and even further. The stage of realization lies far beyond that of liberation.'

'What is realization?' I asked.

Daaji laughed. 'Well, Babuji used to say that if realization can be defined, it is not realization! However you may attempt to define it, it will be something beyond that definition. But to put it in a simplistic way, we can say that realization is to realize the Self within—the core and centre of our being. But is there any difference between our own innermost centre and that of God's manifestation?'

'So realizing the Self is the same as realizing God,' I said.

'Wait and see,' said Daaji. 'Whatever it is, it is the *minimum* qualification that a guru must possess. Otherwise, how can he help us to attain it? The guru's help is required at lower stages as well. There are times in our journey when we arrive at passes that cannot be crossed. It is as if you had been walking nicely through the plains, and now you encounter a deep river. What will you do? So the guru has to take you across. And then, at a very high stage, you become so surrendered to the divine will that you have no more desire to progress. Now, the guru must come again and, like a kangaroo carrying its joey in its pouch, the guru carries you to the next stage. When we finally arrive at the shores of the infinite ocean, we find the guru waiting for us there too, for now he must teach us to swim.

'The guru achieves all of this through transmission, of which he is the custodian. However, a single dose of grace imparted by a guru of calibre can achieve what thousands of transmissions can never do. Again, this happens in a magical way. One has to experience grace to know what it is and to know how it differs from transmission. It is a matter of feeling. Without transmission and grace, the Heartfulness practice has no meaning, and without the guru, there is no transmission, nor is there anyone to channel grace toward the aspirant.'

Just as a currency must be backed by something, so must spiritual practice. Currency used to be backed by gold. Now there is no more gold standard, but currencies have other forms of backing because a currency without backing is valueless. That is the role of the guru—he backs the practice. He is its guarantor—the spiritual gold standard.

Conclusion

FIFTEEN YEARS HAVE passed since my first experience with Heartfulness. What has driven me to continue this practice for all these years? I was completely satisfied on my very first day. What remained for me to pursue? For as much peace and contentment as these last fifteen years have brought, a certain inner restlessness continues to increase. That restlessness comes in response to a silent inner signal in the form of a question:

'Are you what you ought to be?'

There is no external answer to this question. The answer is in the question itself. If I am what I ought to be, the question should not arise. This question is not an expression of despair or helplessness. Rather, it is pregnant with possibility. Without such questions, there can be no evolution.

Transformation is in our hands. Heartfulness

practice provides us with the tools to transform ourselves, but we must choose to use them. To transform yourself is to create yourself anew, starting with the transformation of your inner being. Inner transformation comes automatically, as a result of meditative practice. Without inner transformation, the transformation of our character and lifestyle is only a dream. However, such outer transformation is not automatic. It requires absolute willingness on our part.

The miracle of Heartfulness is that in the very moment we decide to change ourselves, change has already arrived. We don't need to wish for it. We don't need to pray for it. We don't even need to work for it. When we are absolutely willing and open, we need only look within ourselves, and we find that it is already present.

'Are you what you ought to be?'

We can also respond to this question with yet another question: 'How do I know what I ought to be?' Again, there is no external answer. Only your heart can say. But if you are willing to listen, the heart will not remain silent on this matter. Rather, it will gush with answers.

However, even if the heart continuously gives you signals, you will miss them if your mind is as turbulent as the deafening sea. The heart is able to guide us whenever we are in need, but its signals emerge amidst the background noise of our thoughts, emotions, sensations, and other stimuli. When our inner environment is so noisy, how can we perceive the heart's subtle directions?

In order to describe such situations, scientists use the signal-to-noise ratio. This ratio describes the extent to which a desired signal is audible amidst the presence of background noise. For instance, when we tune a radio receiver to a certain frequency, we often hear some static. When there is too much static, the frequency becomes inaudible. The signal has been drowned out by the noise.

The signals within us never shout. They never insist. They come as gently and softly as a whisper. They are not words, but subtle feelings, reflected in the mind as inspired ideas. Unless the mind is silent and still, and unless our emotions are balanced, these signals never surface to our awareness.

Imagine a treasure chest that sits at the bottom of a lake. If only the lake were placid and clear, you would be able to see the golden glimmers under the surface. But the water is rough and filled with sediment, and you cannot see a thing. This lake is the mind, and the treasure chest is the heart.

The waves are our unregulated thoughts, and the sediment is the network of impressions that distort our perception. Only when the mind becomes calm and clear can the heart reveal its secrets. In order for it to become calm, we meditate. In order for it to become clear, we do cleaning. And in order to be receptive to the heart's divine messages, we must maintain an inner attitude of prayerfulness and humility. With a receptive attitude and a mind that is calm and clear, the heart's impulses are automatically translated into inspired thoughts. These inspired thoughts now guide our responses to life's varied circumstances.

Throughout history, human beings have regarded inspiration as something that comes of its own accord, something beyond our conscious control. However, we can make ourselves receptive to it. All we need to do is still the mind through meditative practice. In that sense, meditation is a way to actively cultivate inspiration, which we can then capture.

But what do we do with that captured inspiration? We can use it to respond heartfully to our circumstances, or we can choose to react with the mind instead. Daaji once told me that if we choose to ignore the heart's evolutionary signals, no practice can help us. No guru can help us. Even God cannot help us.

'Why not?' I asked him.

'It is easy to wake up a sleeping person,' he said. 'But no one can wake up a person who is only pretending to sleep!'

If you are responsive to the heart, it speaks to you with progressive clarity. If you ignore its signals, they become weaker and more difficult to perceive. But it is easy to follow the heart! All we need is a little courage and conviction, which arise out of repeated experiences.

The heart's inspirations are always in accord with its nature, which is love itself. The heart will never lead you astray. It will never tell you to rob someone, for instance, or to hurt anyone. Therefore, when living by the heart's inspirations, our actions become effortlessly and automatically good.

At times, the heart inspires us to take positive action. It tells us to help someone, or perhaps, it may give us a new insight. The heart can also assume the form of your conscience and warn you against a negative action. However, it rarely provides positive feedback. As Daaji often says, the heart does not congratulate you for your good deeds!

'Do your lungs congratulate you for breathing normally?' he once asked me.

We only become aware of our breathing when it is laboured. It is a signal that something is wrong. Similarly, the heart will never say, 'Wow, you're doing great stuff!' It simply informs you when you need to change yourself.

Yet, when your orientation in life becomes *evolutionary* in nature, the heart positively vibrates with mystical joy. That is the heart's elation. Its purpose is being fulfilled.

But when is our orientation evolutionary? To answer this question, we must understand something about the heart. The heart is biased toward the common good. A preoccupation with one's own, individual evolution does not move the heart because the heart is not preoccupied with 'self.' The mind thinks *my*, but the heart thinks *our*. The mind thinks *me*, but the heart thinks *we*. To the heart, the universe is a whole.

A spiritual life is one that has come into contact with the universal. In that case, it is not just about 'me'. The stream that has become separate from the river rarely makes it to the ocean. Rather, it stagnates in one place and starts to stink. If we want purpose in our lives—if we want to make it to the shores of the infinite ocean—then we must forget about individual purpose. When I am only concerned for myself, my heart does not cooperate in anything that I do. I have realized this practically in my own life. Purpose is never individual. It is always collective. When we are deeply altruistic in word, deed, and most importantly, intention, our lives assume a different order. We become ennobled. Then our hearts roar into action. So listen to the heart carefully and follow it faithfully. Let it be your inner guru. It will guide you at every step of the way and in every last detail of your life. That is Heartfulness.

EXPERIENCE HEARTFULNESS

To experience Heartfulness:

Visit us at http://www.heartfulness.org or http://www.daaji.org

Like us at https://www.facebook.com/practiceheartfulness/

https://www.facebook.com/kamleshdaaji/

Follow us at https://twitter.com/heartful_ness

https://twitter.com/kamleshdaaji

Email us at info@heartfulness.org

Meditate with us on the Let's Meditate app for Android and iPhone.

Read *Heartfulness Magazine* at http://www.heartfulnessmagazine.com.

Glossary

adi shakti or **aadi shakti**. The original force, or original power, utilized in the process of yogic transmission.

artha. The ways and means of making a living; material prosperity; wealth and power.

asana or **aasana**. Posture; the third stage, or limb, of ashtanga yoga.

ashtanga yoga or **ashtaanga yoga**. Patanjali described yoga as having eight steps, or limbs: yama (good conduct); niyama (regularity, observances); asana (posture); pranayama (breath); pratyahara (inner withdrawal); dharana (mental focus); dhyana (continued attention); and samadhi (original condition, balance).

bhakti. Devotion.

bhoga or **bhogam** or **bhog** or **bhogaa**. The process of undergoing the effects of impressions; experience; enjoyment; suffering.

Brahman or **Brahm**. God, the Ultimate.

dharana or **dharna.** Fixing the mind (sixth limb of Patanjali's yoga).

dharma: A term with many applications, depending on the context: duty, righteousness, destined way, truth, virtue, that which upholds, life of law and justice.

dhyana or **dhyaan**. Continued attention; meditation; the seventh stage, or limb, of Patanjali's ashtanga yoga.

guru: One who transmits light, knowledge; a spiritual teacher.

gyan or **gyana** or **jnana** or **jnaana**. Gnosticism; knowledge.

kama or **kaama**. Desire; love; passion; pleasures and enjoyments.

karma. Action.

mahatma or **mahaatmaa**. Great soul, saint.

moksha. Liberation.

nishkam karma or **nishkaama karma**. Work without attachment to the result; desireless action.

niyama or **niyam**. Second stage, or limb, of ashtanga yoga; observances.

Para Brahman. Indeterminate Absolute; God as the Ultimate Cause of Existence.

pranahuti or **praanaahuti**. Process of yogic transmission; derived from prana, meaning life, and ahuti, meaning offering. Offering of the life force by the guru into the aspirant's heart.

pranayama or **pranayamaa**. Derived from prana (life, vital force) and from ayama (to expand). Hatha yoga breathing technique. Fourth step in Patanjali's ashtanga yoga.

pratyahara or **pratyaahaara**. The inner withdrawal of the sense organs and mind. Fifth step of Patanjali's yoga.

raja yoga or **raaja yoga**: Ancient system or science to realize the Self or God. Usually used for meditative practices, as distinguished from hatha yoga.

samadhi or **samaadhi**. Original balance. State in which we stay attached to Reality; a return to the original condition, which reigned in the beginning. The eighth limb of Patanjali's yoga.

samskara. Impression.

sanyasi, sayasin, or **sannyaasi, sannyaasin**. One who has renounced the world and leads a solitary life of celibacy and asceticism.

shloka. A verse.

sitting. A session of meditation, usually lasting from twenty minutes to an hour, in which the guru or a Heartfulness trainer meditates with a group or an individual for the purpose of cleaning and transmission.

swami (swaami) or **swamiji (swaameeji)**. Hindu priest; saint.

tavajjoh. A Sufi term describing a similar process to yogic transmission.

uparati. Self-withdrawal.

yama. First step, or limb, of ashtanga yoga: self interdiction. Vow of abstinence of violence, falsity, robbery, unchastity, and tendency to acquire.

yoga. A system of philosophy and practice for the sake of uniting the lower self with the higher Self, or God.

yoganidra or **yoganidraa**. A yogi's spiritual state during which they seem to be asleep but they are awake within.

yogi or **yogin**. One who practises yoga; one who achieves union with the Absolute.

Notes

1. Balasubramanian, K.S., Deputy Director of The Kuppuswami Sastri Research Institute, Chennai, India, has kindly confirmed the accuracy of all Sanskrit references and translations.
2. Chandra, R. 2009. *Complete Works of Ram Chandra Volume I.* Kolkata: Spiritual Hierarchy Publication Trust.
3. Vivekananda. 2009. *Complete Works of Swami Vivekananda*. Kolkata: Advaita Ashrama.

A Note on the Authors

Kamlesh D. Patel is an original voice in an ancient tradition. Known widely as Daaji, his teachings arise from his personal experience on the path of Heartfulness, while reflecting his deep spirit of enquiry and respect for the world's great spiritual traditions and scientific advancements.

Joshua Pollock is a Heartfulness trainer and practitioner from the United States. An accomplished Western classical violinist, he has performed and taught throughout the world, and his violin solos can be heard in numerous A.R. Rahman original soundtracks.